GREEN THUMBS: Corn and Beans

**with baby food jars, straws,
egg cartons, and simple things.**

SCIENCE WITH SIMPLE THINGS SERIES

Conceived and
written by

RON MARSON

Illustrated by

PEG MARSON

TOPS LEARNING SYSTEMS

10970 S. Mulino Rd.
Canby, Oregon 97013

ISBN 0-941008-39-8
Library of Congress Catalog Card Number 86-50756

CONTENTS

 **PART I**   **INTRODUCTION**

 **PART II**   **TEACHING NOTES**

 **PART III**   **REPRODUCIBLE STUDENT ACTIVITY SHEETS**

GETTING STARTED

Welcome to *Green Thumbs: Corn and Beans*. Here is a checklist of things to think about and preparations to make, in advance of your first day of teaching.

✏ WHEN TO SCHEDULE

You may teach this module during any season of the year. Corn and beans grow somewhat slower in the dead of winter because of cooler temperatures and reduced daylight hours, but they'll still grow fast enough to meet the scheduling requirements of this module. You can help your plants grow according to schedule by maintaining your classroom within a comfortable temperature range at all times. Under warmer conditions, avoid exposing the plants to long hours of direct sunlight. In cooler environments, set the plants in direct sunlight whenever possible. To compensate for possible slow plant growth, consider planting your own corn and beans a week *before* your students begin FRI/0. (Complete lab FRI/0 steps 1-4, fill the tray with vermiculite, then moisten and add seeds.) Later on, any student with plants that lack the requisite maturity for a particular experiment, can transplant one of your head starts into their own tray.

Consult your school calendar before you start this module. Begin on Friday, followed by 4 uninterrupted weeks of 5 days each. If your schedule isn't blessed with that many continuous days, its easier to miss days near the end of the 4-week period than near the beginning. It is not possible to teach this module on an alternating M/W/F or Tu/Th schedule. There is too much to do, to observe, and to record. If you have an alternating schedule, consider rearranging it: Teach science on a daily basis for one entire month at the expense of some other subject; then make up the lost subject by teaching it the following month at the expense of science.

It is unusual to begin a new TOPS module on the last day of a school week, but necessary. What you accomplish on Friday sets the stage for a running start the following Monday. The corn and beans have an entire weekend to soak up water and germinate; students have their plant journals cut out, assembled and ready to use.

If you find it necessary to adapt this module down to lower ability levels, consider having students assemble most equipment the week *before* growing starts. This might include journals: FRI/0 steps 7-15, balances: lab TUE/4 steps 2-17, and pole planters: lab WED/5 steps 2-14. Students can thereby proceed at a slower pace and still keep up with their growing plants.

✏ WHERE TO GROW

Full-spectrum indirect daylight that enters your room through outside windows is sufficient to grow corn and beans. Narrow spectrum fluorescent lighting will not support normal photosynthesis. Exposure to direct sunlight, while beneficial, is not necessary. It may even be harmful if the plants are not well-watered.

Any horizontal surface on a window side of your classroom makes a suitable growing area. Table tops, ledges, shelves, even the floor will serve. Only modest amounts of growing space are needed. All experiments in this module fit on a single sheet of notebook paper. That's less than 1 square foot of space per lab group.

Estimate available growing space in your room by laying down sheets of notebook paper, side by side, over all suitable storage surfaces. If you lay down more papers than the total number of students in your class, then you have sufficient space to organize lab groups of one student each. This will engage all of your students most effectively in the learning process. Working independently, each one gets to do all phases of every experiment.

You can cut your space requirements in half by assigning students to work in cooperative pairs. All students are still responsible for keeping personal plant journals, but they team up in twos to work through lab instructions and to share growing trays, jars and balances.

Avoid organizing lab groups larger than 2 members, or pairing a dominant and a passive student. Consider which students work most cooperatively together, then pair them by writing both names at the top of a set of lab pages (see next paragraph). If students prefer to work alone, or need to work alone, let them do so.

✏ WHAT TO COPY

☐ 10 LAB PAGES: Find these at the beginning of the reproducible activities section in this book. They are numbered lab 1, lab 2, ..., lab 10, in the lower right corner of each page. Duplicate and collate these sheets in sequence, in 10-page sets, *one for each lab group* in your class, plus a few extras. Staple each set in the upper left corner, both front and back, to prevent the back pages from working loose. Pencil in the name(s) of each student or student pair you've chosen to form a lab group at the top of the first page. Don't use pen. You'll want to recycle these lab instructions next time you teach this module. When you distribute these instructions on FRI/0, tell students they are for reference only. They should use them as they would any textbook, returning pages unmarked and in good shape at the end of the module.

☐ 12 JOURNAL PAGES: Find these in the reproducible activities section, right after the lab pages. These are numbered journal 1, journal 2, ..., journal 12, in the lower right corner of each page. Duplicate and collate these sheets in sequence, in 12-page sets, *one for each student* in your class, plus a few extras. Paper clip (don't staple) each set in the upper left corner. Hand these out on FRI/0 as well. Students will ask for them soon after you have distributed the lab pages. (Note: To speed journal assembly, one teacher reports that she makes just *one* plant journal, then photocopies class sets of each page *already* attached to notebook paper. If you try this, it may be necessary to darken the notebook paper lines on your journal master for clear reproduction.)

☐ 1 TAKE-HOME TEST: Find this at the end of the book, right after the journal pages. Duplicate *one for each student* in your class, plus extras. Paper clip these together and save until FRI/28, the last day of this module.

✏ WHAT TO GATHER

Once you gather the simple materials listed on the next page, you're ready to begin a great educational adventure, an integration of science, math, language and drawing.

GATHERING MATERIALS

You hold within your hands a **complete teaching resource**. This book contains 21 days of reproducible science lessons, together with all necessary information to help you teach each new day successfully. All you add are the simple materials listed at the bottom of this page.

Look it over. This modest collection of materials is **all** you need to teach every lesson. You probably already have many items. Get the rest from your local supermarket, and have your students bring what they can from home.

This TOPS module is different from most others, because nearly all materials are needed early on. After the first 3 days, few new items will be introduced. This makes our usual summary of materials at the end of each new lesson redundant and unnecessary. Gather everything now, **before** you start the first lesson.

Needed quantities depend on several factors: how you teach, how many students you have, and how you organize them into activity groups. The numbers listed by each item correspond to the main teaching strategies in use today. Find the option that corresponds to your teaching situation, and gather quantities accordingly.

Once you collect all necessary materials, place them on an equipment table or open shelves that are accessible to your students. Items of special interest (rubber bands, for example) may require closer supervision in your desk drawer.

Many of the materials listed below are used in other TOPS modules as well. As you continue to teach different modules and build a TOPS inventory of often-used materials, you'll find that gathering new materials requires less and less effort.

Q¹

Resource Center
Activity Corner
Parent-Child Activity
Demonstrations

Quantities are sufficient for 1 student or lab group to complete all of the activities. If you multiply Q¹ by a factor of 2, then there will be enough material for 2 groups working simultaneously on the same activity.

Tending plants and keeping journal notes requires a daily commitment of time. If you plan to use this module in an activity corner, be sure to allow your students enough time every day so they can keep pace with their growing plants.

Q²

Individualized Approach

The ideal way to study science is to learn independently, to move through the lessons at your own pace. But in this module, individualized study and flexible scheduling are severely restricted by the subject matter.

Corn and beans grow at their own pace. Students and teachers have no choice but to follow along, doing experiments when the plants are ready, interpreting results when there are results to see. Because individualized learning is not a viable option, quantities for Q² remain unlisted.

Q³

Traditional Class Lessons

If you want all your students to study corn and beans, then everyone needs to stay together. Begin as a group on Friday, then continue together on a daily basis over the next 4 weeks.

Quantities in Q³ assume a class size of 30 students working in groups of 2. This makes 15 lab groups. Modify these numbers as necessary to fit your own number of lab groups.

MATERIALS

Q¹ / Q³

1 / 30	pairs of scissors
25 / 750	sheets of notebook paper — college ruled preferred, wide ruled OK
1 roll / 4 rolls	clear tape
1 / 1	stapler
1 pkg / 1 pkg	pinto beans — sold in grocery stores
1 pkg / 1 pkg	popcorn — sold in grocery stores
2 / 30	baby food jars with lids — double quantities if you plan to send plants home with students (see "clean-up" notes for THU/27)
1 / 1	water source
1 roll / 2 rolls	masking tape
1 / 15	styrofoam egg cartons — if unavailable, substitute other containers (see note 1 for FRI/0)
1 roll / 6 rolls	paper towels
1 / 15	wide-mouth jars — pints or larger
10 / 150	paper clips
4 / 60	straight plastic straws
6 / 90	straight pins
1 / 15	tin cans — medium sized
1 qt / 15 qts	vermiculite — sold in garden and variety stores
3 / 45	wooden clothespins
1 / 1	spool of thread
1 / 1	jar of petroleum jelly
1 / 15	size D batteries — dead ones OK
1 btl / 2 btls	blue food coloring — use self-dispensing bottles or provide eyedroppers
2 / 30	wide rubber bands
1 / 15	large paper grocery bags (optional) — use only if you plan to send plants home with students (see "clean-up" notes for THU/27)
1 pkg / 1 pkg	lentils — sold in grocery stores; use for Take-Home Test
1 pkg / 1 pkg	wheat berries (whole grains of wheat) — sold in health food or farm stores; use for Take-Home Test

DIARY OF A TEACHER

THE DAY BEFORE

Tomorrow is the first day of school. With anxiety and anticipation you check to see that everything in your classroom is in good order.

You have already duplicated 30 copies each of the first few lessons in this TOPS module. They lay on your desk, each in a manila folder marked with large numbers 1, 2 and 3. You make a mental note to bring a large box and a brick to school tomorrow. These will prop the folders upright like a vertical file, and help keep you organized as you add additional folders.

You wonder how you ever managed without manilla folders. Already you have printed each student's name on a fresh new assignment folder and stapled a sheet of graph paper to the inside cover to track each student's progress. When they arrive tomorrow, you will surprise them with a worksheet, a file folder and the simple instruction, "Get busy". You've already laid out the necessary materials on a table in the back of your room. You smile inside yourself; you haven't felt quite this prepared in years.

DAY 10

Your class has been humming now for 10 straight days. Perhaps not humming: buzzing more aptly describes the state of orderly confusion. Students have questions and problems to be sure. (You wish they would at least *read* the instructions before running to you for an explanation.) Still, the worksheets provide a firm sense of direction. Students know where they are and understand where they need to go.

Now that students understand your system, they come to class and get straight to work on what they were doing the day before. Just before lunch they tend to quit early, but at other times you have to pry them away from their experiments. You tell the slower ones to assign themselves homework to catch up and it seems to be working!

The assignment folders work well too. Students point with pride at the growing list of check-points you have marked off on their graph paper progress charts. As their folders expand so does their self confidence.

DAY 15

Today 2 groups of students who seem to be racing each other have completed all 20 activities. The bulk of your class remains 3 to 6 activities behind, with a few stragglers plus the new kid bringing up the rear.

You announce that individualized worksheet activity will end in 2 days. The most advanced students seem eager to work on several experiments of their own. You can follow that up with an "Extension" activity if time allows. You help the slow ones catch up by assigning three key-concept activities while skipping the rest.

There is a frenzy of activity as students rush to meet your deadline. They know that part of their grade is determined by the total number of activities they complete.

DAY 18

Today you kick back and relax. You have assigned several students to give reports on their original investigations. The rest of the period will be taken up with a film. For tomorrow you've planned a blackboard review of major module concepts. Then on Friday you'll finish off with an exam.

The kids are already bugging you about grades and asking what they will be studying next. You decide to give them a 3-part grade weighted equally on pace (number of lessons completed), attitude, and the exam. As to what they'll study next, you can't decide. Perhaps you'll let *them* decide.

Its already the fourth week into the school year and you don't even feel the strain. Activity-centered teaching seems so natural and easy. You respond to questions that kids have instead of the other way around. You ask yourself why you never taught this way before.

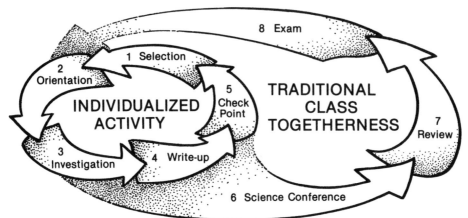

1. SELECTION. Students generally select worksheets in the order you specify. They should be allowed to skip a task that is not challenging, however, or repeat a task with doubtful results. When possible, encourage students to do original investigations that go beyond or replace particular activites.

2. ORIENTATION. Good students will simply read worksheet instructions and understand what to do. Others will require further verbal interpretation. Identify poor reader in your class. When they ask, "What does this mean?" they may be asking in reality, "Will you please read these instructions aloud?"

3. INVESTIGATION. Students observe, hypothesize, predict, test and analyze, often following their own experimental strategies. The teacher provides assistance where needed and the students help each other. When necessary, the teacher may interrupt individual activity to discuss problems or concepts of general class interest.

4. WRITE-UP. Worksheets ask students to explain the how and why of things. Answers should be brief and to the point. Students may accelerate their pace by completing these out of class.

5. CHECK POINT. The student and teacher evaluate each write-up together on a pass/no-pass basis. If the student has made reasonable effort consistent with individual ability, the write-up is checked off on a progress chart and included in the student's personal assignment folder kept on file in class.

6. SCIENCE CONFERENCE. After individualized activity has ended, students come together to discuss experiments of general interest. Those who did original investigations give brief reports. Slower students learn about the later activities completed only by faster students. Newspaper articles are read that relate to the topic of study. The conference is open to speech making, debate, films, celebration, whatever.

7. REVIEW. Important concepts are discussed and applied to problem solving in preparation for the module exam.

8. EXAM. Evaluation questions are written in the teaching notes that accompany each activity. They determine if students understand key concepts developed in the worksheets. Students who finish the test early begin work on the first activity in the next new module.

GAINING A WHOLE PERSPECTIVE

Science is an interconnected fabric of ideas woven into broad and harmonious patterns. Use the ideas presented below to help your students grasp the big ideas — to appreciate the fabric of science as a unified whole.

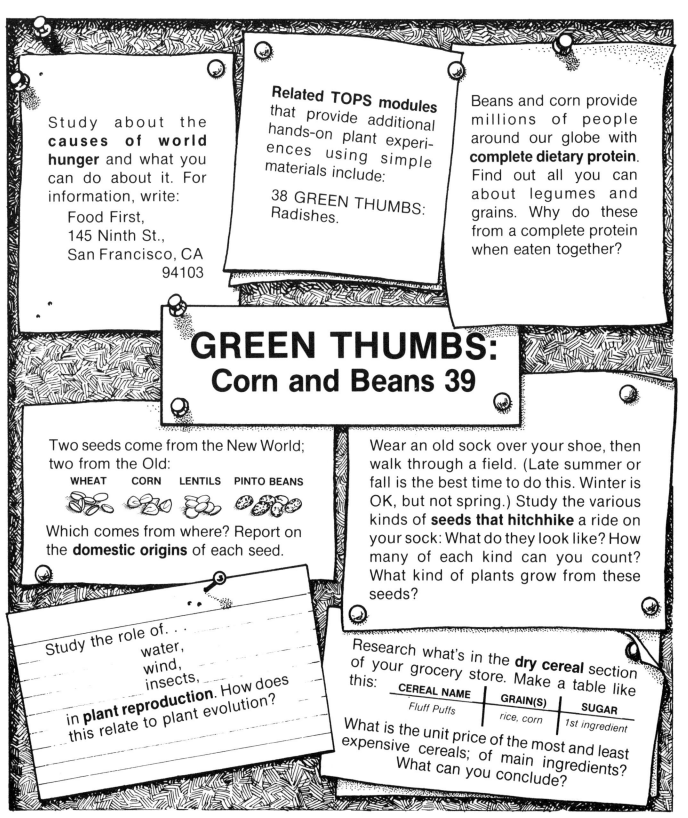

Study about the **causes of world hunger** and what you can do about it. For information, write:

Food First,
145 Ninth St.,
San Francisco, CA
94103

Related TOPS modules that provide additional hands-on plant experiences using simple materials include:

38 GREEN THUMBS: Radishes.

Beans and corn provide millions of people around our globe with **complete dietary protein**. Find out all you can about legumes and grains. Why do these from a complete protein when eaten together?

GREEN THUMBS:
Corn and Beans 39

Two seeds come from the New World; two from the Old:

WHEAT   CORN   LENTILS   PINTO BEANS

Which comes from where? Report on the **domestic origins** of each seed.

Wear an old sock over your shoe, then walk through a field. (Late summer or fall is the best time to do this. Winter is OK, but not spring.) Study the various kinds of **seeds that hitchhike** a ride on your sock: What do they look like? How many of each kind can you count? What kind of plants grow from these seeds?

Study the role of. . .
water,
wind,
insects,
in **plant reproduction**. How does this relate to plant evolution?

Research what's in the **dry cereal** section of your grocery store. Make a table like this:

CEREAL NAME	GRAIN(S)	SUGAR
Fluff Puffs	rice, corn	1st ingredient

What is the unit price of the most and least expensive cereals; of main ingredients? What can you conclude?

LONG-RANGE OBJECTIVES

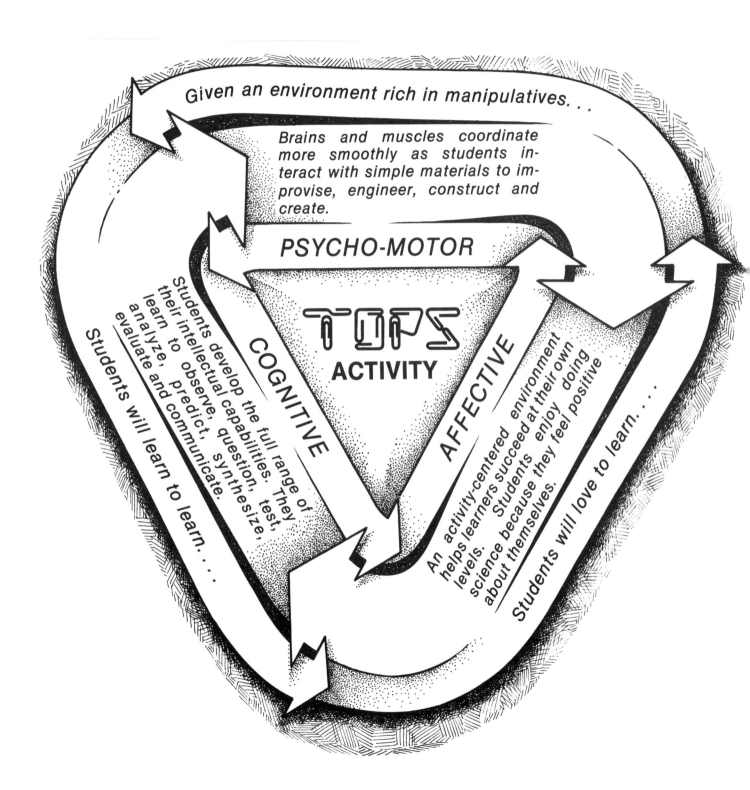

Given an environment rich in manipulatives. . .

Brains and muscles coordinate more smoothly as students interact with simple materials to improvise, engineer, construct and create.

PSYCHO-MOTOR

TOPS
ACTIVITY

COGNITIVE

Students develop the full range of their intellectual capabilities. They learn to observe, question, test, analyze, predict, synthesize, evaluate and communicate.

Students will learn to learn. . . .

AFFECTIVE

An activity-centered environment helps learners succeed at their own levels. Students enjoy doing science because they feel positive about themselves.

Students will love to learn. . . .

E

TEACHING NOTES

FRI/0 through FRI/28

NAME: _____

LAB INSTRUCTIONS

4 weeks
10 pages

lab FRI/0

**Make an egg carton seed tray

1 Cut away the bumps on an egg carton lid. Tape your name(s) to the side.

"SAW" WITH SCISSORS
NAME

2 Fold 2 paper towels in half 3 times lengthwise. They should be no wider than 2 fingers.

2 FINGERS WIDE

3 Push both towels halfway through the center hole. Set them in a widemouth jar filled with water.

TOWELS JUST TOUCH BOTTOM
← WATER

4 Lay back 1 towel on each side. Fold a third in half to cover the entire bottom.

THIRD TOWEL

5 Spread out 18 pinto beans and 9 corn in your tray. Cover with a fourth folded towel.

FOURTH TOWEL

6 Soak with more water. Close the lid and set aside.

A sprout nursery!

*Make your plant journal

7 Get 12 journal cut-outs from your teacher.

8 Cut around the dashed lines into 23 separate parts:

Count them!
19 WEEKDAYS . . . . . plus 4 PAPER MASSES.

9 Paper clip the 4 paper masses together, and set aside.

10 Tape each weekday to a new sheet of notebook paper, even with the upper right corner.

a. TAPE LEFT SIDE
b. TAPE AROUND RIGHT EDGE
journal MON/3   journal MON/10

11 Arrange all 19 journal days in order, beginning with MON/3. Add a cover sheet.

19 plus a cover.

12 Tap the edges even. Staple very near each hole like this:

STAPLES
EVEN EDGES
CONTINUE

This module is organized by weekdays, not lesson numbers. The number appearing after each weekday expresses the total elapsed time (in days) since the corn and beans were first exposed to water. Thus "FRI/0" means the seeds are introduced into a damp environment on Friday. "MON/3" means that on Monday, a total of 3 days will have have elapsed since that event, and so on. These numbers do *not*, of course, refer to dates in the calendar month. FRI/0 can happen on any Friday of any month in the year. No need to wait till the Zero of Never!

The double asterisk in front of the first heading has meaning only if you've paired at least some of your students into lab pairs. It suggests that 2 students work together with shared materials, producing a single seed tray between them. The single asterisk in front of the second heading suggests that individuals work alone, even though paired in a lab group. Thus each student makes a separate plant journal.

**Make an egg carton seed tray

1. A half-gallon milk carton made of waxed cardboard may be substituted if styrofoam egg cartons are unavailable. Fully open its top, then cut it in half top to bottom, forming a tray (end pinched closed with masking tape) and a lid (end left open).

3. Wide-mouth jars provide maximum stability. Quart jars are good; large peanut butter jars are even better.

6. Keep the lid closed when not observing your seeds. This reduces cooling by evaporation and speeds germination.

*Make your plant journal

8. This step is labor-intensive. To expedite the cutting process, furnish *every* student with a pair of scissors. Borrow extras from across the hall if you have to. Soon your classroom will be awash in confetti. Place extra waste baskets or paper bags about your room to manage the waste.

After they finish cutting, remind your students to count all their separated pieces. If they count fewer than 19 weekdays or 4 paper masses, they have neglected to separate all pieces. (Journal page 9 is often missed because it separates into 3 parts.) Incomplete separation must be discovered now, otherwise students will complain of missing pages during final journal assembly in step 11.

10. Each student will need 2 pieces of clear tape per cut-out, or 38 total pieces. Conserving tape to only 1/2 inch per piece. (as wide as the nail on your index finger). still consumes 19 inches total (use your arm as a measuring stick). How do you cope with a classroom of students all needing so many tiny pieces of tape at the same time? Easy. Circulate about your room distributing single 19-inch strips as student ask for them. Tear each long piece off the roll and lay it flat across their desk, with a paper clip under one end. Tell students to cut more managable pieces from the longer strip. They should cut these to 1/2 inch lengths, storing them along the edge of their desk. Always keep the paper clip at the end of the longer piece to make it easy to pick up.

Tape each cut-out flush with the top-right corner of the notebook paper, keeping to the right of the 3 binder holes. This way, the staples will only have to penetrate a managable 20 sheets of notebook paper.

11. Students should follow this sequence: FRI/0, MON/3, TUE/4, . . ., THU/27. Weekends, of course, are always missing.

12. Before stapling, make sure all pages are pressed together evenly, forming a uniform spine. Back pages, in particular, have a tendency to fan off center and miss the staple. Because the margin for error between the holes and paper edge is somewhat slim, consider asking younger students to bring their assembled journals to your desk for final stapling.

15. The last step in today's activity is numbered "15." But the reduced student lab page to the right goes up only to number "12." We couldn't organize this module by our customary pattern of just one activity page per day because so many lab steps (today's boxes 13, 14 and 15, for example) spill over to a second page.

Before you do anything else, take an extra set of 10-page lab instructions you have already copied, and write your own name at the top. Tuck it inside this book to use as a permanent co-reference. From now on, *no* more lab instructions will be reduced and printed to the right. Whenever you wonder what a particular teaching note is describing, consult these companion lab instructions for clarification. Beginning with MON/3, on the page below, all teaching notes follow a daily *journal* format, not a daily *lab* format.

lab	1	2	3	4	5	6	7	8	9	10	11	12
journal												

The **BEAN** is covered by a speckled **seed coat**. It protects the plant embryo, wrapped inside, from insects and water loss. The scar where the bean was once attached to its pod is called the **hilum**. Next to the hilum is a tiny hole called the **micropyle**. The embryo absorbs water most rapidly through this opening.

The largest part of the **CORN** is a yellow fruit called the **endosperm**. It is a food source for the white **embryo**, living inside, that will grow into a corn plant.

Locate, label and define these parts.

Seed coat :

A covering for the plant embryo; it keeps water in and insects out.

micropyle :

A small hole that allows water to pass rapidly into the embryo.

hilum :

The scarred point of attachment of the bean to its pod.

embryo :

The living part of the seed that grows into a plant.

endosperm :

A food storehouse for the embryo.

EXTEND LINES DOWN FROM ALL ARROWS

11

List below 4 ways your dry bean and corn seeds are **different**.

1. *The bean is more rounded, the corn more angular.*

2. *The bean is colored in shades of brown, the corn in shades of yellow.*

3. *The bean is about 2 times a large as the corn.*

4. *The bean embryo is hidden from view but the corn embryo is visible.*

12

List 4 ways your dry bean and corn seeds are similar.

1. *Both seeds are covered by a hard, smooth coat.*

2. *Both seeds have white points of attachment.*

3. *Both seeds contain living embryos inside surrounded by a source of food.*

4. *Both seeds have the potential to germinate and grow into plants.*

END

TEACHING NOTES

Notice how this page corresponds visually with the first double page in your students' plant journals. Model answers are all filled in, to use as an answer key. These teaching notes generally refer to the 10-page set of lab instructions you added on FRI/0. that now form a permanent co-reference with the rest of this book. This page and ones that follow, reproduce in miniature a fully-completed student journal.

Before your class begins today's activity, review the function of the "score box" at the top of each journal page. Point out that it functions as a guide between lab directions and written journal responses. Today, MON/3 for example, begins with 10 lab steps and ends with journal steps 11 and 12. Tomorrow, TUE/4, begins in the journal, jumps to the lab then back again, and finally ends in the lab. It's easy to stay on track in this module if you follow the "score box" as a kind of road map.

*Make a bean map

1. Trace *both* the square *and* the 2 bean patterns inside.

3. A small percentage of pinto beans have seed coats that are unusually dark. A few may be especially small or unusual looking beans. The idea here is to avoid unusual looking beans, so that students will have to rely on the accuracy of their bean maps (step 4) to find their special beans again in a "crowd" (steps 5-6).

4. Good representational drawings require a slow, deliberate hand that draws exactly what the eye sees. Praise those who carefully capture the intricate seed coat patterns on their special beans. Encourage your class to exercise similar care in all future drawings they will make in their journals.

**Soak some new seeds

8. These seeds will absorb water and soften over the next 2 days, making them suitable for dissection on WED/5.

*Draw your sprouts

9. This step marks the beginning of a 4-week tradition. Every day your class will sketch their most advanced bean and corn plants. These are now in the form of sprouts. Later they will rapidly grow into plants. Set a "bean-map" standard of excellence now, and hold your students to it throughout this module. They will reward you (and themselves) with their best effort. In 4 weeks they'll have an entire journal filled with wonderful work, something to take home and proudly show family members.

IMPORTANT: If you require a daily check point to enforce high standards now, you'll avoid long hours of journal grading later. Your initials at the top of each day's journal page could signify that each page has passed inspection. At the end of this module. when it comes time to grade the entire journal, a quick count of all the pages you've initialed will enable you to easily quantify a final grade.

Tell your class how you plan to grade. If they perceive your initials as valuable, and you tell them that you only initial current work, students will come to you on a daily basis to ask you to look at their journals. They'll seek you out; you won't have to seek them.

*Look at the outside

10–12. If time is short, you can assign the rest of today's journal as homework. Besides their journals, students need take home only a dry bean and corn seed for reference. Stress the importance of returning journal to class the next day.

3-DAY-OLD SPROUTS :

lab																							
journal	1	2	3	4	5	6	7	8	9	10	11	12	13	14	15	16	17	18	19	20	21	22	23	24

*Draw your sprouts

1 Draw your fastest-growing bean and corn sprout on the left page.

LAB

19 Compare the mass of dry seeds to soaked seeds on your balance, then complete each equation:

ALWAYS CENTER FIRST

5 soaked beans = _10-11_ dry beans

5 soaked corn = _6-6½_ dry corn

20 Draw in these boxes the differences you notice:

DRY BEAN → SOAKED BEAN

DRY CORN → SOAKED CORN

21 Describe these before/after changes, using **complete** sentences.

DRY ...before adding water	WET ...after 24 hours
SIZE	
BEAN: *It is about 2 lines of notebook paper long; a little more than 1 line wide.*	BEAN: *It has expanded to perhaps twice its original volume.*
CORN: *It fits snugly inside a notebook paper hole.*	CORN: *Its volume has increased only slightly.*
COLOR	
BEAN: *The seed coat is light brown, covered with dark brown, irregular spots.*	BEAN: *Light and dark brown patterns remain, but have faded dramatically.*
CORN: *A deep yellow, translucent endosperm surrounds a nearly white embryo.*	CORN: *The yellow endosperm is now lighter and more opaque.*
TEXTURE	
BEAN: *It is hard and smooth.*	BEAN: *It is soft and feels slightly sticky; when squeezed water appears.*
CORN: *It is hard with well-defined angles and and ridges.*	CORN: *It is still hard; but the surface is now round and smooth.*

TEACHING NOTES

*Draw your sprouts

1. With only a few exceptions, students routinely record each new day of plant development on the left page. Insist that these daily drawings be the best that each student can produce. Good drawings here will carry over into the rest of the journal as well, and into each student's class work in general.

**Build a balance

2-3. To make an unbiased balance, it is critical to push the pin through the center of the straw, so each side has nearly the same length. Check pin placements, if necessary, and reposition any that are off-center. Circle your corrected pin hole so students will know which one to use in step 8.

11. The straw won't yet balance level, though some students may think that it should. Move them on to step 12 and tell them not to worry. All beams will eventually balance when centered in step 17.

12. You can dramatically reduce wasted foil by pretearing pieces off the roll for student use.

To transfer the image of the rectangle, simply place the foil underneath while

tracing around the rectangle's perimeter with a pencil. The pencil will leave an impression in the foil that is easy to follow and cut out. It will also leave a mark in the reference-only lab journals. This is OK.

17. Most balances will already balance close to a centered position. The tape rider, therefore, should be cut relatively small.

From this centering step, the directions proceed directly to step 18 on the next line; then over to the journal and back again. Remind students to follow the sequence outline at the top of their journal page to avoid confusion.

**Make a storage mat

23. This single sheet of notebook paper defines all the storage space that each lab group requires for the duration of this entire module.

24. This balance will be used extensively later. In another week, on TUE/11, students will cut out paper gram masses to begin an entire series of quantitative weighing activities. Until then, these balances should remain inactive on the storage mats. Assure impatient students that in due time they will have many opportunities to use the wonderful instruments they have just made.

4-DAY-OLD SPROUTS:

lab		2	3	4	5	6	7	8	9	10	11	12	13	14	15	16	17	18		
journal	1																		19	20

*Draw your sprouts

⟨LAB⟩

✏ **1** Draw your fastest-growing bean and corn sprout on the left page.

The **BEAN** embryo easily breaks apart into **two cotyledons**. These store starch and protein, enabling the **plumule** to grow into the first 2 true leaves and the **radicle** to develop into the roots and lower stem.

The white **CORN** embryo does not divide easily because it has only **one cotyledon**. It absorbs starch and protein that is stored in the yellow **endosperm** for growth and development.

radicle ___ :
Becomes the roots and lower stem; a part of the embryo.

plumule ___ :
Becomes the first 2 true leaves; a part of the embryo.

two cotyledons ___ :
Store starch and protein for growth and development; part of the embryo.

one cotyledon ___ :
Absorbs food from the endosperm for growth and development; part of the embryo.

endosperm ___ :
A reserve of starch and protein; separate from the embryo.

"MONO" means "ONE".
"DI" means "TWO".

19 Which seed above is called a "**monocot**" (monocotyledon)? Explain.

20 Which seed is called a "**dicot**" (dicotyledon)? Explain.

⟦END⟧

The corn is a monocot because it has only 1 cotyledon.

The bean is a dicot because it has 2 cotyledons.

▌TEACHING NOTES▐

**Make a pole planter

2-5. Wrapping the paper clip in tape, and sandwiching it between layers of sticky masking tape, provides a firm anchor for the long bean pole constructed in steps 5-14.

6. Use notebook paper that has the same line width as the plant journal. Mixing a "college-ruled" pole with a "wide-ruled" journal, for example, would enlarge the plant drawings a little beyond actual size.

7. It is essential to double the notebook paper *in half* 4 times in succession, forming 16 layers. This yields a stiff, narrow "pole" only 1 finger wide.

11. Students habitually number their papers *above* the line. It will take extra effort and explaining on your part to get them to depart from this norm and number *through* the line. Remind students as well to number up (not down), and to count the crack between both pieces of paper as 1 line.

14. This tie should not interfere with the bean's cotyledons. If the cotyledons happen to grow opposite line 20, and remain there, raise or lower the tie out of the way.

*Look at the inside

16-17. All 5 beans and 5 corn wrapped in the damp towel are available for dissection. Students may inadvertently damage some of these in the process of learning how to open them cleanly. Corn is especially difficult to split open because it has only 1 cotyledon.

Unused seeds and fragments can be discarded or returned to the tray as students wish. If returned to the covered moist tray, students may be surprised to notice that even half seeds sometimes grow — a poignant demonstration of life force.

5-DAY-OLD SPROUTS:

lab		2	3	4	5	6	7
journal	1						

*Draw your sprouts

LAB

1 ✎ Draw your fastest-growing bean and corn sprout on the left page.

The lower half of the **BEAN** radicle develops into a complete root system: The **primary root** first grows down into the ground seeking moisture. The hard **root cap** at the tip protects it from being torn apart as it pushes through the soil. Tiny tubes called **root hairs**, just visible along the sides, absorb extra water. These are soon replaced by branching **secondary roots** that absorb water and anchor the plant firmly in the soil. With the root system in place, the **hypocotyl** directly above lengthens into a lower stem, pulling its **two cotyledons** through the soil into open sunlight.

CORN also develops a **primary root**, **root cap** and **root hairs** similar to the bean. Then the **coleoptile** pushes up from its **one cotyledon**. It forms a hollow protective tube that encloses the leaves safely inside until they can grow above ground. Meanwhile, **adventitious roots** grow form the base of the coleoptile to further support the plant and absorb water.

hypocotyl :
Forms the lower stem; pulls the cotyledons above ground as it lengthens.

two cotyledons :

primary root :
The first root to grow down; absorbs moisture.

secondary roots :
These branch out from the primary root, replacing the root hairs. They absorb moisture and anchor the plant.

root hairs :
Numerous tiny tubes on the primary root that absorb extra water.

root cap :
A hardened shield that protects the tip of the primary root as it pushes down.

adventitious roots :
These branch out from the base of the coleoptile, well above the primary root. They absorb moisture and anchor the plant.

coleoptile :
Wraps the leaves like a protective sheath until it grows above ground.

one cotyledon

root tip

root hairs

primary root

END

TEACHING NOTES

Plant your pole planter

2-4. This rolled up paper towel functions as a water sensor. When it wicks up enough water to feel damp to the touch, the vermiculite holds sufficient water as well. When it feels dry to the touch, its time to add more water to the vermiculite before it drys out as well.

Vermiculite holds water like a sponge. In all but the driest climates, there is a margin of safety of several days between the time the paper towel first dries out and the vermiculite inside the jar finally dries out.

Because it is so easily compressed, the jar should be filled brim-full with vermiculite,

but never packed down. Over time some settling will occur naturally.

4-5. Hold the jar nearly upside down so excess water drains away completely. The vermiculite sticks very well to itself. It will not fall out of the jar. If the pencil holes in step 5 back-fill with water, drain the jar more thoroughly.

6. The tip of the bean and corn should just barely poke above the surface. Even though these plants may not grow significantly over the next 24 hours, students can still draw the tips of the seeds when they sketch their pole planters for the first time on FRI/7.

6-DAY-OLD
SPROUTS :

journal FRI/7

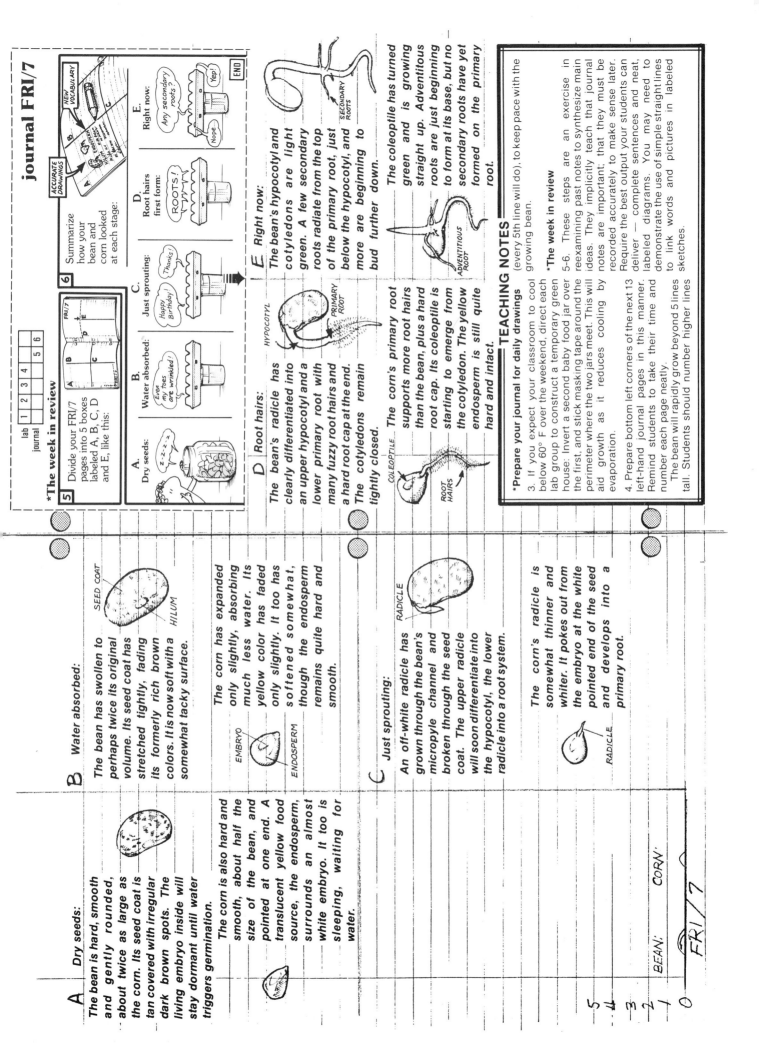

ACCURATE DRAWINGS

NEW VOCABULARY

END

6 Summarize how your bean and corn looked at each stage:

D. Root hairs first form:
ROOTS!

C. Just sprouting:
Happy Birthday!
Thanks!

E. Right now:
Any secondary roots?
Nope...
Yep!

lab	1	2	3	4		
journal					5	6

5 Divide your FRI/7 pages into 5 boxes labeled A, B, C, D and E, like this:

A. Dry seeds:
z-z-z-z

B. Water absorbed:
Even my toes are wrinkled!

E | Right now:

The bean's hypocotyl and cotyledons are light green. A few secondary roots radiate from the top of the primary root, just below the hypocotyl, and more are beginning to bud further down.

HYPOCOTYL

PRIMARY ROOT

SECONDARY ROOTS

The coleoptile has turned green and is growing straight up. Adventitious roots are just beginning to form at its base, but no secondary roots have yet formed on the primary root.

ADVENTITIOUS ROOT

D | Root hairs:

The bean's radicle has clearly differentiated into an upper hypocotyl and a lower primary root with many fuzzy root hairs and a hard root cap at the end. The cotyledons remain tightly closed.

COLEOPTILE

The corn's primary root supports more root hairs than the bean, plus a hard root cap. Its coleoptile is starting to emerge from the cotyledon. The yellow endosperm is still quite hard and intact.

ROOT HAIRS

TEACHING NOTES

(every 5th line will do), to keep pace with the growing bean.

3. If you expect your classroom to cool below 60° F over the weekend, direct each lab group to construct a temporary green house: Invert a second baby food jar over the first, and stick masking tape around the perimeter where the two jars meet. This will aid growth as it reduces cooling by evaporation.

4. Prepare bottom left corners of the next 13 left-hand journal pages in this manner. Remind students to take their time and number each page neatly.
The bean will rapidly grow beyond 5 lines tall. Students should number higher lines

5-6. These steps are an exercise in reexamining past notes to synthesize main ideas. They implicitly teach that journal notes are important; that they must be recorded accurately to make sense later. Require the best output your students can deliver — complete sentences and neat, labeled diagrams. You may need to demonstrate the use of simple straight lines to link words and pictures in labeled sketches.

A | Dry seeds:

The bean is hard, smooth and gently rounded, about twice as large as the corn. Its seed coat is tan covered with irregular dark brown spots. The living embryo inside will stay dormant until water triggers germination.

SEED COAT

HILUM

The corn is also hard and smooth, about half the size of the bean, and pointed at one end. A translucent yellow food source, the endosperm, surrounds an almost white embryo. It too is sleeping, waiting for water.

EMBRYO

ENDOSPERM

B | Water absorbed:

The bean has swollen to perhaps twice its original volume. Its seed coat has stretched tightly, fading its formerly rich brown colors. It is now soft with a somewhat tacky surface.

The corn has expanded only slightly, absorbing much less water. Its yellow color has faded only slightly. It too has softened somewhat, though the endosperm remains quite hard and smooth.

C | Just sprouting:

An off-white radicle has grown through the bean's micropyle channel and broken through the seed coat. The upper radicle will soon differentiate into the hypocotyl, the lower radicle into a root system.

RADICLE

The corn's radicle is somewhat thinner and whiter. It pokes out from the embryo at the white pointed end of the seed and develops into a primary root.

RADICLE

BEAN: CORN:

0 1 2 3 4 5

lab														
journal	1	2	3	4	5	6	7	8	9	10	11	12	13	14

LIKE A
HOOK:

LEAVES
INSIDE:

*Pole planter

[1] Get your pole planter. On the left page, carefully draw how high both seedlings now reach up the pole.

[2] Next to your drawing, explain why the bean's **hypocotyl** forms a hook; why the corn's leaves hide inside a **coleoptile**.

←LAB

*Draw your sprouts

[3] Accurately draw your most advanced bean and corn sprout in the space below. Label all parts.

FASTEST
GROWING!

LABEL ALL PARTS...

CORN:

BEAN:

adventitious roots

coleoptile

cotyledon

primary root

root
hairs

root cap

hypocotyl

cotyledons

secondary
roots

root
hairs

primary
root

root
cap

▬ TEACHING NOTES

*Pole Planter

1. Depending on temperature and hours of daylight, your sprouts may have grown halfway up the pole by now, or they may still be in the ground. Either way, on this and each new day, students should draw exactly what they see of the plants, sketching in as much detail as possible.

2. If the bean's hypocotyl and the corn's coleoptile have not yet emerged, direct students to look inside their closed seed trays to find more developed examples.

**Plant your seed tray

4. Numerous roots have likely grown through the top towel into the water-wicking towels underneath. This tends to bind both towels together. Many of these roots will release, perhaps a few will tear, as you gently pull the top towel free.

6. Only the top towel needs to be replaced. The 2 towels that extend into the water underneath should remain, *unless* they are moldy. If mold has grown, throw all 3 towels away. Thoroughly rinse the jar and fill it with clean water before replacing the towels.

7. Each plant needs to be pulled firmly yet gently until its roots are finally dragged free of the towel. Some roots will unavoidably break, but the plants can easily grow new ones.

Notice that only *dry* vermiculite is added to the tray. Don't moisten with water until you completely fill the tray in step 10. Once soggy, vermiculite is extremely difficult to work.

8. So far, only enough dry vermiculite fills the tray to stand 6 bean plants and 4 corn plants more or less upright. The right quarter of the tray still has no vermiculite at all.

Any left-over sprouts that look healthy might be planted in a special container of moist vermiculite that you prepare in advance. These would insure against future calamity and crop loss. (Throw away

infertile seeds and runts to prevent molding.) Students who want to take their sprouts home should place them in the egg-cup portion of the tray they cut off in step 5, cover them with a moist paper towel, and transplant into soil as soon as they reach home.

9. The new seeds added here, and later in step 2 of WED/12, insure a continuous supply of new sprouts for later experiments, regardless of fast or slow growing conditions in your particular classroom.

11. The seed tray is now somewhat less stable because it carries a heavier load of soaked vermiculite. The paper clips, braced against opposite sides of the jar, prevent the tray from sliding off center.

14. Beans require extra support once they grow beyond the horizontal straw. There are several ways to prop them up: (a) Unbend a paper clip, then use it to link plants together on opposite sides of the straw. (b) Bend straight pins to right angles. Stick them into the straw (not through it) wherever they are needed. (c) Fashion ties from masking tape, similar to the ones you made in steps 13–14 of WED/5. (d) Tape commercial vegetable twist-ties to the straw.

(a)

(b)

(c)

(d)

Demonstrate some of these possibilities to your class. Your students might invent other methods as well.

The bean's hypocotyl is hooked so it can pull its 2 cotyledons out of the soil without breaking them open.

The corn's coleoptile penetrates the soil like a spear, protecting the structurally fragile leaves inside until they can poke through into the air and sunshine above.

4

3

2

1

0

MON/ 10

journal TUE/11

lab		3	4	5		
journal	1	2			6	7

*Pole planter

1 On the left of this page, draw how high both seedlings now reach up the pole planter.

2 Divide the 2 columns you drew below into 4 boxes, labeled A, B, C and D. Answer each of these questions in its own box.

A. Observe your growing plants. Do they grow straight up, or lean in a favored direction? Make a drawing.

B. Propose a theory to explain your observations.

C. How might you test your theory?

LAB

END

**Weigh a seed

6 Weigh a dry bean and corn on you balance. Tell how you did this in box **D** below.

7 Store all paper masses inside the can.

A *All bean and corn plants without exception lean towards the window.*

B *Plants are stimulated by sunlight. They respond by growing towards it. By increasing their exposure to light, they increase their capacity to photo-syntheize and grow. (This effect, known as a "phototropism", is studied in greater detail in Green Thumbs: Radishes #38.)*

C *Here are 2 ways to test this theory:*
(1) Turn the plants halfway around to lean in the opposite direction. See if they grow back towards the light again.
(2) Grow some plants in a dark closet. Compare their size and direction of growth with plants raised in sunlight.

D *To find the mass of a seed, first center your balance beam to a level position. Then place the seed in the left bucket and add paper masses to the right paper clip until the beam again balances level. Total the paper masses to determine the weight of the seed.*
A dry bean typically ranges between 300 and 450 mg.
A dry corn typically ranges between 100 and 160 mg.

TEACHING NOTES

*Cut out your paper masses

3. We have sized these paper masses for reproduction onto 20 pound bond or 50 pound book stock. Both of these paper grades are nearly equivalent, and commonly used in copy machines. Even if your particular copy paper weighs a little heavier or lighter, all experimental results will still remain internally consistent, as long as you use don't mix grades of copy paper.

Caution students to cut out these paper masses with extra care. Any time their scissors stray off the line, they'll be subtracting weight from one mass standard while adding that same amount to a neighboring mass standard.

balance? The answer is "no" of course, but some students may intuitively disagree. Whether the foil is flattened over a wide area, or fashioned into a more compact bucket, the same amount of aluminum is always present. Mass is conserved.

**Weigh a seed

6. To write clear directions that are easy to understand, we have used the terms "mass" and "weight" interchangably, as in normal English usage. We don't think your students will be mislead by this kind of talk. When they are intellectually ready, you can teach them that mass is a measure of how much material an object contains; that an object exhibits weight in a gravitational field. On Earth, we naturally speak of mass and weight interchangably because our gravitational field is reasonably constant.

5. It is more manageable (believe it or not) to slip the paper weights between a flattened piece of foil and its paper clip, than to roll up the paper weights and load them inside the 3-dimensional bucket.

Pose this problem to your class: A balance is centered so that 2 buckets originally balance level. Will smashing one of them flat upset this original state of

7. If students are working in lab pairs rather than individually, they'll cut out an extra set of paper masses. Tell them to hold these in reserve by paper clipping them to a back reserve journal page. These can be used as needed to replace masses that are damaged by water or lost.

TUE / 11

10
9
8
7
6
5
4
3
2
1
0

lab journal	1	2	3	4	5	6	7	8

*Pole planter

1 On the left page, draw each pole plant exactly as you see it—like a snapshot. LAB

5. Here is one result. Data tables will vary widely, of course.

TABLE:	#1	#2	#3	#4	TOTAL	AVERAGE
DRY BEAN	340	410	360	390	1500	375
DRY CORN	140	150	110	120	520	130

... all data in milligrams

6 After you weigh all 8 seeds, soak them overnight under water. 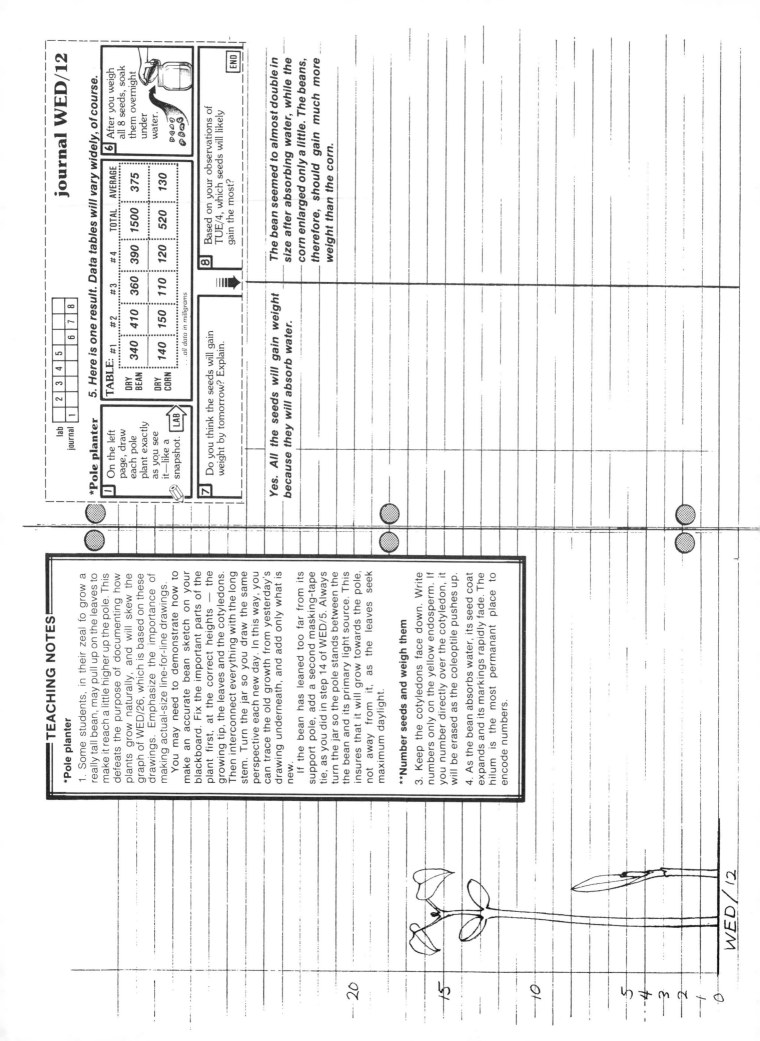 END

7 Do you think the seeds will gain weight by tomorrow? Explain.

Yes. All the seeds will gain weight because they will absorb water.

8 Based on your observations of TUE/4, which seeds will likely gain the most?

The bean seemed to almost double in size after absorbing water, while the corn enlarged only a little. The beans, therefore, should gain much more weight than the corn.

TEACHING NOTES

*Pole planter

1. Some students, in their zeal to grow a really tall bean, may pull up on the leaves to make it reach a little higher up the pole. This defeats the purpose of documenting how plants grow naturally, and will skew the graph of WED/26, which is based on these drawings. Emphasize the importance of making actual-size line-for-line drawings.

You may need to demonstrate how to make an accurate bean sketch on your blackboard. Fix the important parts of the plant first, at the correct heights — the growing tip, the leaves and the cotyledons. Then interconnect everything with the long stem. Turn the jar so you draw the same perspective each new day. In this way, you can trace the old growth from yesterday's drawing underneath, and add only what is new.

If the bean has leaned too far from its support pole, add a second masking-tape tie, as you did in step 14 of WED/5. Always turn the jar so the pole stands between the the bean and its primary light source. This insures that it will grow towards the pole, not away from it, as the leaves seek maximum daylight.

**Number seeds and weigh them

3. Keep the cotyledons face down. Write numbers only on the yellow endosperm. If you number directly over the cotyledon, it will be erased as the coleoptile pushes up.

4. As the bean absorbs water, its seed coat expands and its markings rapidly fade. The hilum is the most permanent place to encode numbers.

20

15

10

5
4
3
2
1
0

lab					
journal	1	2	3	4	5

*Pole planter

1 Draw each pole plant exactly as you see it. Your sketch should always show the height of leaves **and** cotyledons.

**Weigh soaked seeds

2 Complete this table. Use your balance, plus data from WED/12:

	#1	#2	#3	#4	Total	Average
SOAKED BEAN	690	810	710	780	2990	748
DRY BEAN	340	410	360	390	1500	375
Water Absorbed	350	400	350	390	1490	373
SOAKED CORN	180	200	150	170	700	175
DRY CORN	140	150	110	120	520	130
Water Absorbed	40	50	40	50	180	45

...all data in milligrams

3 Fold a **wet** paper towel into the bottom of a baby food jar, and set your 8 seeds on top.

4 Use data from your table to compare how beans and corn absorb water. Was your prediction from WED/12 a good one?

5 Tape on your name. Cover tightly and set aside until MON/17.

How many beans are needed to absorb 250 grams of water? (1 gram = 1000 mg)

END

one glass full!
250 mg

(Answers will vary. Encourage as much math analysis as possible.)

GOOD ANSWER: The beans absorbed an average of 373 mg of water per seed, while the corn only absorbed 45 mg of water per seed. As predicted yesterday, the beans gained far more weight than the corn.

BETTER ANSWER: The beans absorbed an average of 373 mg of water. This represents almost a 100% increase in mass:

$$\frac{373}{375} \times 100 = 99\% \ increase$$

The corn absorbed, on average, only 35% of its dry weight in water.

$$\frac{45}{130} \times 100 = 35\% \ increase$$

As predicted yesterday, the beans absorbed far more water than corn, by virtue of both their greater absorbing capacity and their larger size.

(If this problem is too difficult for younger students, try working it on the board as a class exercise.)

An average bean absorbs 373 mg of water. Making a rough estimate, 3 beans absorb about 1000 mg of water, or 1 gram. Thus 3 X 250 beans would absorb a whole glassful. More exactly,

$$\frac{1 \ bean}{373 \ mg} \times \frac{1000 \ mg}{1 \ g} \times \frac{250 \ g}{1 \ glass} = 670 \ \frac{beans}{glass}$$

TEACHING NOTES

*Pole planter

1. The bean will soon grow higher than the journal page, if it hasn't done so already. When this happens, advise students to split their bean drawing into two parts as shown: the lower bean to the left (from ground level to above the cotyledons); the upper bean to the right (from above the cotyledons to the top of the plant).

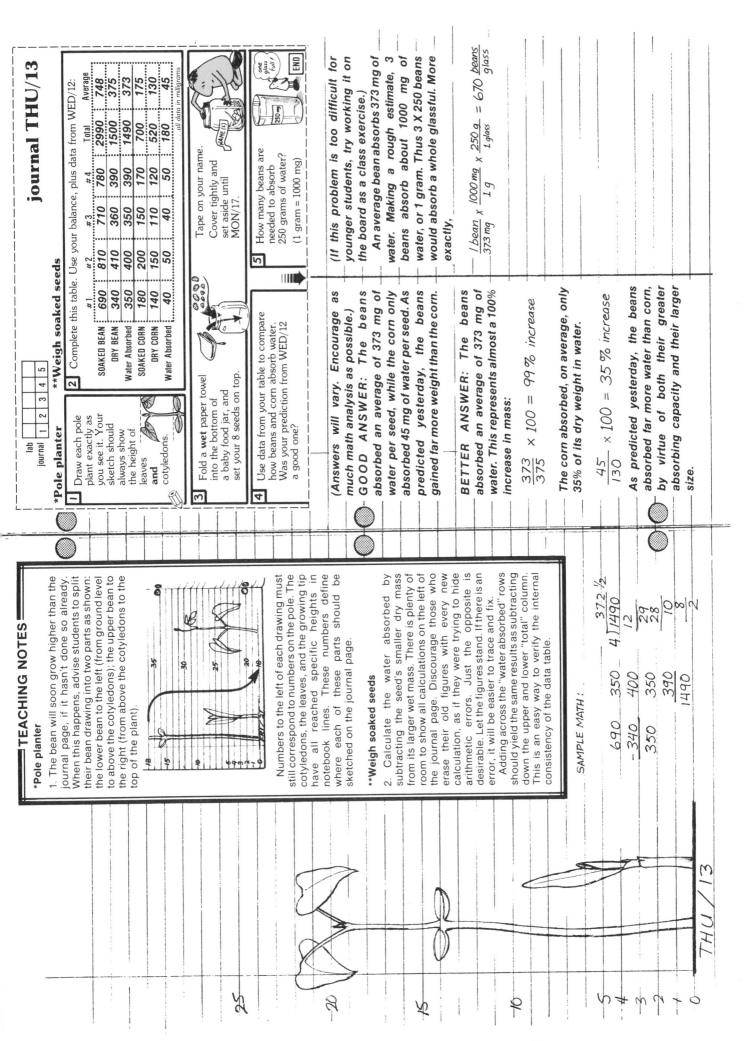

Numbers to the left of each drawing must still correspond to numbers on the pole. The cotyledons, the leaves, and the growing tip have all reached specific heights in notebook lines. These numbers define where each of these parts should be sketched on the journal page.

**Weigh soaked seeds

2. Calculate the water absorbed by subtracting the seed's smaller dry mass from its larger wet mass. There is plenty of room to show all calculations on the left of the journal page. Discourage those who erase their old figures with every new calculation, as if they were trying to hide arithmetic errors. Just the opposite is desirable. Let the figures stand. If there is an error, it will be easier to trace and fix.

Adding across the "water absorbed" rows should yield the same results as subtracting down the upper and lower "total" column. This is an easy way to verify the internal consistency of the data table.

SAMPLE MATH:

```
  690      350      400            372 1/2
- 340    - 400    - 350         4)1490
  350      350      390            12
                                   29
                   390             28
                  1490             10
                                    8
                                    2
```

THU / 13

LAB ✏

lab		2	3	4	5	6	7		
journal	1							8	9

*Pole planter

1 Accurately draw on the left page how both plants have gained height.

8 Leaves turn green in sunlight as they use the sun's energy to photosynthesize their own food.

Green!

Predict the color of your leaf after being covered for a long time with foil. Explain your reasons.

9 Leaves breathe in air through tiny openings (stomata) in their leaves. Stomata are too small to see without a microscope.

CO_2 O_2

If grease plugs these holes, the leaves can't breathe. How might this experiment tell us where the stomata are located?

END

The part of the leaf covered by foil won't receive sunlight. Thus it can't photosynthesize, and will lose its green color. It will likely turn yellow, as leaves do in the fall when they die.

That part of the leaf with plugged stomata won't be able to breathe or carry on photosynthesis. Again, over time, it will likely turn yellow and die. If "B" yellows but "T" remains green, then the stomata must be located only on the bottom. If "B" remains green but "T" yellows, then the stomata must be located only on the top. If no part of either leaf dies, perhaps the experiment hasn't run long enough, or the stomata are located on both sides. If both parts on each leaf die, perhaps the petroleum jelly is toxic for some other reason.

TEACHING NOTES

**Add water

2. Water the corn and beans now so they don't dry out over the weekend. Caution students not to overwater their pole planters. If the beans and corn end up standing in water, tip the jar over a sink to drain away any excess. Wet vermiculite sticks to itself; only water will spill out of the jar.

**Cover some bean leaves

7. Be sure your class understands the purpose of this experiment before you allow them to grease up their fingers. Otherwise they typically grease *both* sides of the leaves, sacrificing it entirely. Grease once applied cannot be removed.

30

25

20

15

10

5
4
3
2
0

FRI/14

	lab journal	1	2	3	4	5	6	7	8	9	10	11

*Pole planter **Sprout mass

1 Accurately draw how both plants have grown.

[LAB]

9 Complete this mass table. Be sure to center your balance first . . .

	DRY WED/12	SOAKED THU/13	SPROUTED MON/17
BEAN #4	390	780	1090
CORN #2	150	200	230

(milligrams)

Return both sprouts to their jar so each leans against the damp towel. Keep water in the bottom; the lid tightly closed.

[END]

10 How much **more** mass did each seed gain after the 24-hour soak of THU/13?

⟹

11 What **other** way can seedlings gain mass besides absorbing water?

The seedlings can turn green and begin photosynthesizing their own food.

The bean gained 310 mg of additional mass, while the corn gained 30 mg.

BEAN:
$$1090 - 780 = 310$$

CORN:
$$230 - 200 = 30$$

**Sprout mass

9. The mass of the thread is negligible compared to the mass of the whole sprout. It can be safely ignored, but students should be aware they are doing so.

When weighing wet sprouts, a certain amount of moisture will remain inside the balance cup. It is especially important,

therefore, to recenter the balance after each weighing. This will also insure that good results are obtained for the graph of TUE/25, which is based on this data.

This experiment runs more risk of running dry than any other. Even with the lid tightly closed, water still evaporates off the exposed water, wicking water from inside the jar to the outside.

TEACHING NOTES

**Tie a bean and corn sprout

2-5. Out of this collection of 8 sprouts, only 1 bean and 1 corn need to be tied. All untied survivors can be either discarded, taken home or added to the discard tray you may have created in step 8 of MON/10.

3. The bean's hypocotyl is easy to tie with thread. But great care must be taken not to pull the knot too tightly. This will cut the hypocotyl in two, or seriously weaken it so it breaks off later. To underscore this point more dramatically, ask any volunteer to describe how it feels to have a thread loop pulled too tightly around the finger.

4. If the corn's coleoptile has poked above its surrounding endosperm, as illustrated, it will prevent the thread loop from slipping off the tapered end of the seed when it is drawn closed and knotted. But if the top surface of the embryo is still smooth, the loop will merely slip off the end of the seed each time you tighten the thread.

For undeveloped corn seeds another method of attachment is clearly needed:

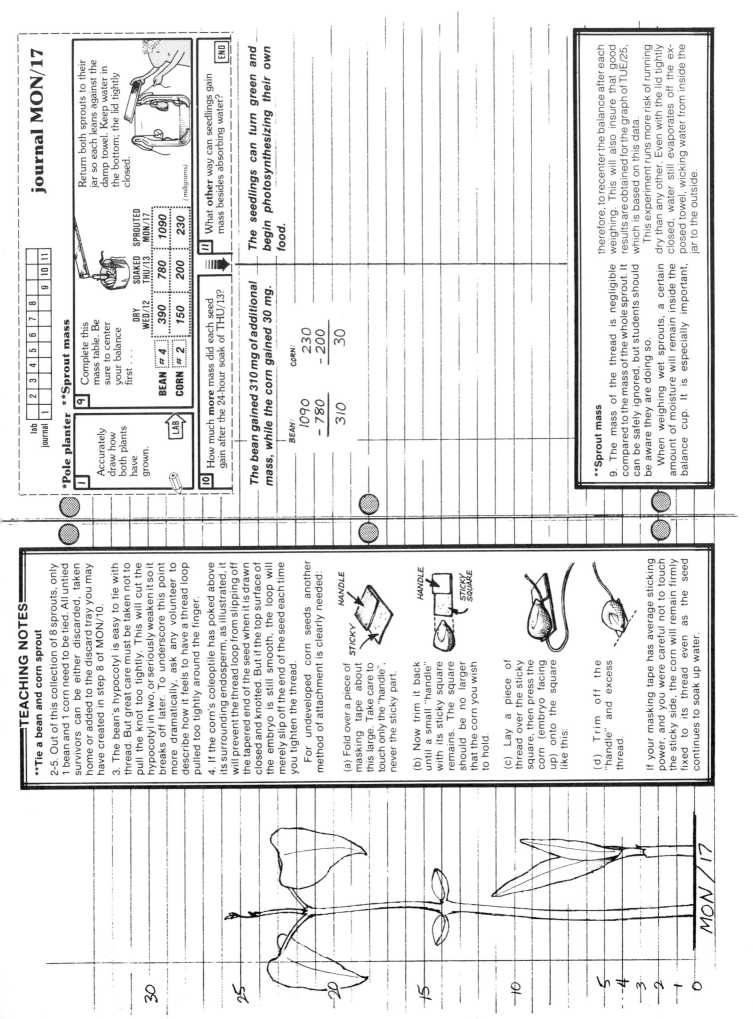

(a) Fold over a piece of masking tape about this large. Take care to touch only the "handle", never the sticky part.

HANDLE STICKY

(b) Now trim it back until a small "handle" with its sticky square remains. The square should be no larger that the corn you wish to hold.

HANDLE STICKY SQUARE

(c) Lay a piece of thread over the sticky square, then press the corn (embryo facing up) onto the square like this:

(d) Trim off the "handle" and excess thread.

If your masking tape has average sticking power, and you were careful not to touch the sticky side, the corn will remain firmly fixed to its thread even as the seed continues to soak up water.

5
4/25
3
2
1
0
MON / 17

30
25
20
15
10

lab journal	1	2	3	4	5	6	7	8	9	10	11

*Pole planter

1 Accurately sketch how both plants have gained height.

**Sprout mass

2 Weigh each sprout you tied with thread.

	(in milligrams)
BEAN SPROUT	1270
CORN SPROUT	220

Return them to their jar and close the lid.

**Compare roots

3 Gently uproot a young bean and corn plant from your tray. Rinse off the roots.

CAREFUL!

4 Divide your columns below into boxes labeled 5, 6, 7 and 8. Do each step in its own box.

5 Sketch the bean's root system. Use this key:
PRIMARY ROOT
SECONDARY ROOT

BEAN

6 Sketch the corn's root system. Use this key:
PRIMARY ROOT
SECONDARY ROOT
ADVENTITIOUS ROOT

CORN

LIKE THESE

7 Describe how these root systems are similar.

8 Describe how these root systems are different.

LAB

Both the corn and bean have a single, well-developed primary root, with many secondary roots branching off in all directions along its entire length.

The secondary roots of the corn are all relatively short and even, compared to its long, thick primary root. The bean has longer, better-developed secondary roots branching off near the top of its primary root. These thin out and become smaller near the tip of the primary root.

The corn has adventitious roots growing above the primary root, from the base of the coleoptile or stalk. The bean develops no equivalent kind of root at all.

TEACHING NOTES

**Compare roots

3. Select young corn and bean plants as illustrated, with only 2 developed leaves per plant. Older root systems are too complex and difficult to draw.

*Compare leaves

9. Use leaves from the uprooted corn and bean plants you have already sacrificed.

11. Tomorrow's lesson depends on your students bringing monocot and dicot leaves to class. Write this assignment on your blackboard for emphasis. Gather examples yourself, to share with those who forget.

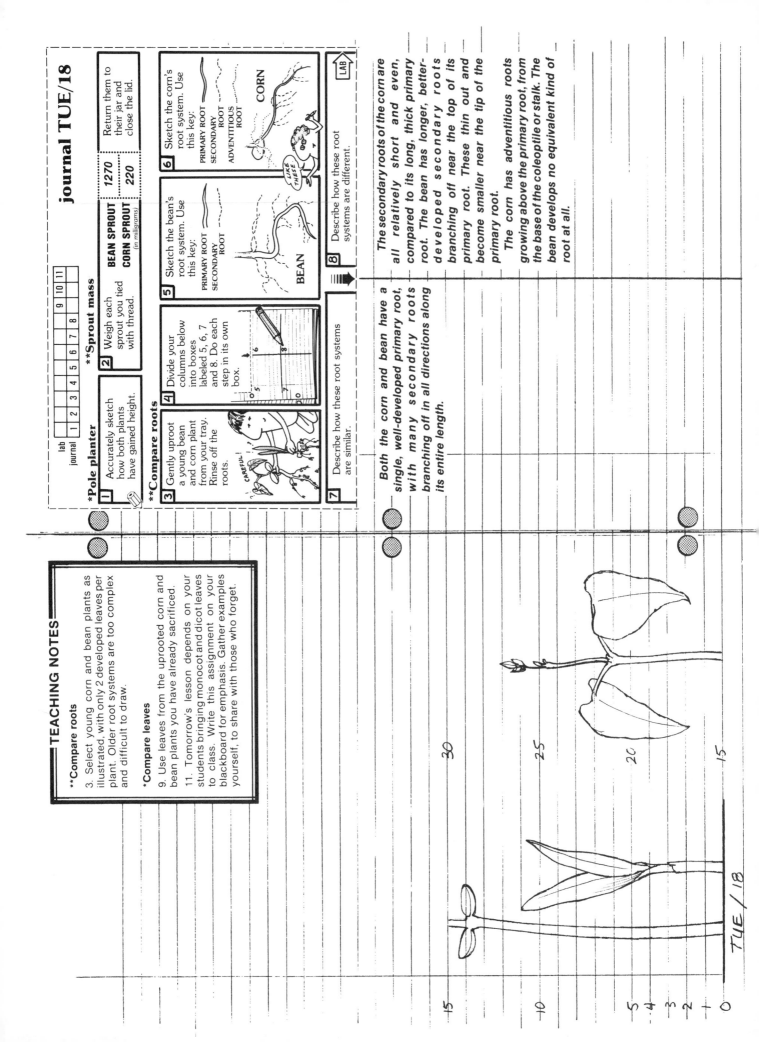

30

25

20

15

15

10

5
4
3
2
1
0

TUE / 18

TEACHING NOTES

*Monocots and dicots

3-4. Flowering plants divide into 2 broad groups — dicots and monocots. There are roughly 200,000 species of dicots and 50,000 species of monocots. If time allows, go outside and identify examples growing in your school yard. Every true leaf you encounter must be one or the other. Classify any seeds you can find as well. Such a trip might result in a great bulletin board display.

Do you see a fir or spruce tree growing nearby? These are called "polycots" because their female cones contain not 1 or 2 covered seeds (angiosperms), but many naked seeds (gymnosperms).

lab					
journal	1	2	3	4	5

*Pole planter

1 Accurately sketch how both plants have gained height.

*Monocots and Dicots

3 Cut out the rubbings you made yesterday. Tape each into the correct column below.

CUT:

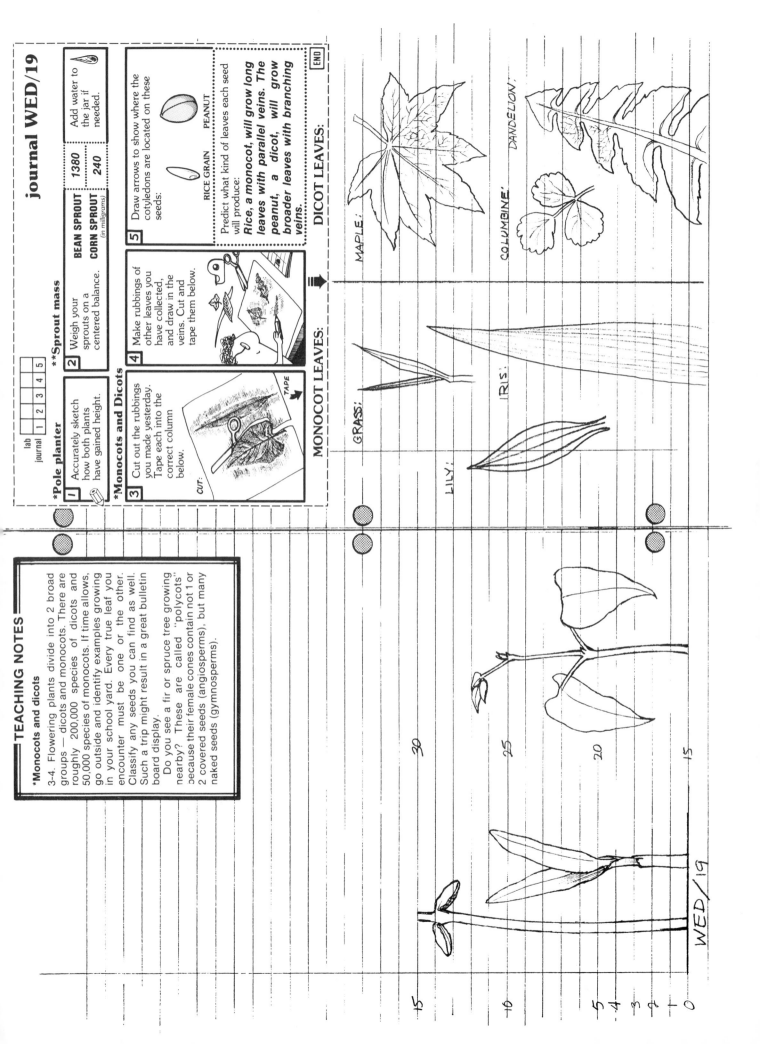

TAPE

**Sprout mass

2 Weigh your sprouts on a centered balance.

4 Make rubbings of other leaves you have collected, and draw in the veins. Cut and tape them below.

Sprout mass

BEAN SPROUT	*1380*
CORN SPROUT	*240*

(in milligrams)

Add water to the jar if needed.

5 Draw arrows to show where the cotyledons are located on these seeds:

RICE GRAIN   PEANUT

Predict what kind of leaves each seed will produce:

Rice, a monocot, will grow long leaves with parallel veins. The peanut, a dicot, will grow broader leaves with branching veins.

END

DICOT LEAVES:

MAPLE:

COLUMBINE: DANDELION:

MONOCOT LEAVES:

GRASS: LILY:

IRIS:

WED/19

30

25

20

15

15

10

5
4
3
2
0

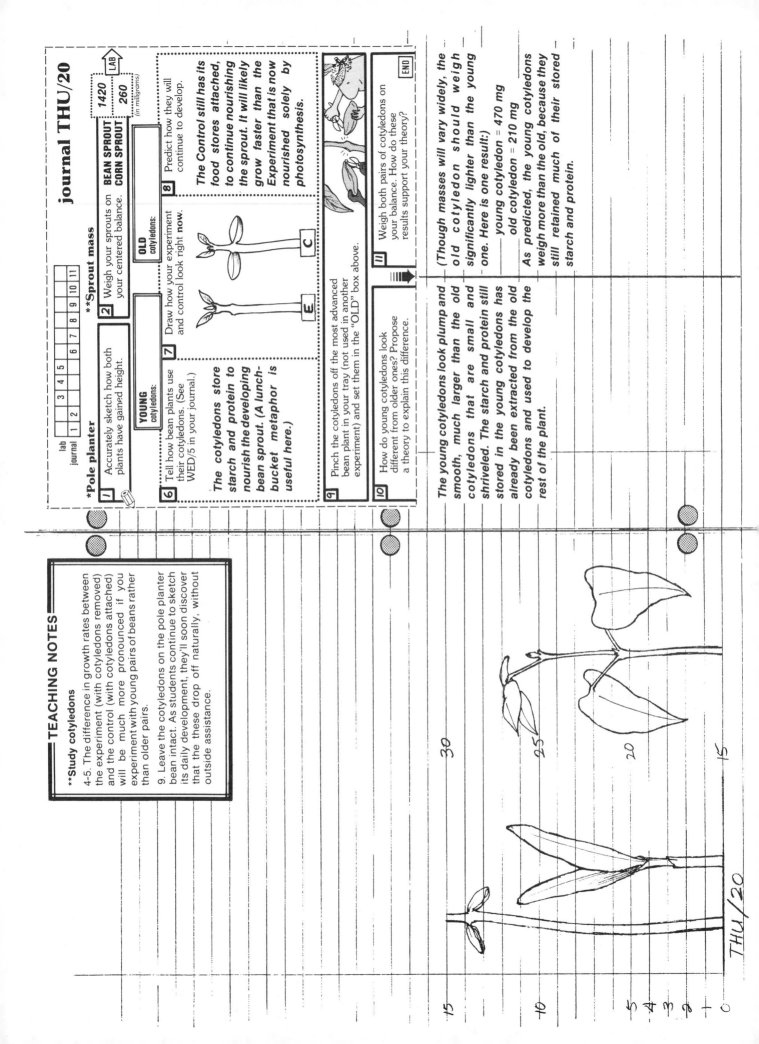

journal THU/20 → LAB

Sprout mass

| BEAN SPROUT | 1420 |
| CORN SPROUT | 260 |

(in milligrams)

*Pole planter   **Sprout mass

lab journal	1	2	3	4	5	6	7	8	9	10	11

1 Accurately sketch how both plants have gained height.

2 Weigh your sprouts on your centered balance.

6 Tell how bean plants use their cotyledons. (See WED/5 in your journal.)

The cotyledons store starch and protein to nourish the developing bean sprout. (A lunch-bucket metaphor is useful here.)

7 Draw how your experiment and control look right now.

YOUNG cotyledons: OLD cotyledons:

E   C

8 Predict how they will continue to develop.

The Control still has its food stores attached, to continue nourishing the sprout. It will likely grow faster than the Experiment that is now nourished solely by photosynthesis.

9 Pinch the cotyledons off the most advanced bean plant in your tray (not used in another experiment) and set them in the "OLD" box above.

10 How do young cotyledons look different from older ones? Propose a theory to explain this difference.

11 Weigh both pairs of cotyledons on your balance. How do these results support your theory?

END

The young cotyledons look plump and smooth, much larger than the old cotyledons that are small and shriveled. The starch and protein still stored in the young cotyledons has already been extracted from the old cotyledons and used to develop the rest of the plant.

(Though masses will vary widely, the old cotyledon should weigh significantly lighter than the young one. Here is one result:)
  young cotyledon = 470 mg
  old cotyledon = 210 mg

As predicted, the young cotyledons weigh more than the old, because they still retained much of their stored starch and protein.

TEACHING NOTES

**Study cotyledons

4-5. The difference in growth rates between the experiment (with cotyledons removed) and the control (with cotyledons attached) will be much more pronounced if you experiment with young pairs of beans rather than older pairs.

9. Leave the cotyledons on the pole planter bean intact. As students continue to sketch its daily development, they'll soon discover that the these drop off naturally, without outside assistance.

30   25   20   15

15 10 5 4 3 2 1 0

THU/20

journal FRI/21

lab												
journal	1	2	3	4	5	6	7	8	9	10	11	12

*Pole planter

1 Accurately sketch how both plants have gained height.

**Sprout mass

2 Weigh your sprouts. Remember to center your balance before you begin.

	(in milligrams)
BEAN SPROUT	1490
CORN SPROUT	290

**Add water

3 Add water to your pole planter, plant tray, and sprout jar for the weekend.

[LAB]

8 This "corn plant" has been marked with food coloring dots 1 line apart. Practice marking the "bean stem" in the same way with your pin and food coloring.

CORN:

BEAN:

9 As both plants continue to grow, predict how each section will change (or not change). Give reasons for each answer.

a. tip-top of bean:

The spots will no longer reach to the very tip-top, because new growth will reach above them.

b. upper bean stem:

The spaces between all the spots will increase, as cells already formed continue to lengthen.

c. tip of new leaf to mid-coleoptile:

The space between the coleoptile's top and the leaf's bottom will widen most, because the corn leaf grows from its base, not its tip.

d. lower coleoptile:

There will be little or no widening of the spaces here, because the lower coleoptile is relatively old, and its cells are already fully grown.

10 Mark a bean and corn plant in your tray that look similar to the drawings above.

NOW: (Show the dots)

11 On the left, draw how your plants look **now**.

12 On the right, draw how they will look **later**, based on your predictions above.

[END]

LATER:

NEW CELLS

LARGER CELLS

NO CHANGE

NEW CELLS PUSHING UP

TEACHING NOTES

**Add water

3. If the sprouts seem ready to outgrow their covered jar, give them extra growing room: remove the lid, throw away the side towels, and stand both plants in sufficient water to last the weekend.

**Study plant growth

4. Conserve notebook paper by encouraging students to share the same piece, or use scratch paper. It would be a shame to sacrifice several dozens sheets of notebook paper with a single "bite" taken out of each one.

a. New stem cells were added to the top.

b. All existing stem cells grew a little longer.

c. New stem cells were added at the bottom, pushing older growth up.

8. To mark spaces 1 line wide, always line up either edge of the paper with the last dot to determine the position of the next dot. The pin head will likely need to be "reinked" after each spot is applied.

9. To stimulate speculation about how plants grow, draw a thin straight plant stem marked at equal intervals on your blackboard. Label it "before." Then draw 4 possible growth outcomes and label these "after." For each case, discuss where new cells were added; where old cells enlarged.

10. Select plants that are likely to grow rapidly over the weekend. A good choice for the corn is one with a newly emerging second leaf. Find a bean with 2 leaves fully deployed and a middle shoot pushing up perhaps a centimeter in the middle.

BEFORE a. b. c.
— AFTER —

EVEN SPACES:

NOW:

FRI/21

*Pole planter

**Sprout mass

lab journal	1	2	3	4	5	6	7	8

BEAN SPROUT	1890
CORN SPROUT *(in milligrams)*	320

Add water to the jar if needed.

1 Accurately sketch how both plants have gained height.

2 Weigh your sprouts:

*How plants grow

Mark off equal spaces with a pen to represent "cells" in a plant stem.

3 Cut a thick rubber band to make a single strand . . .

4 Hold the rubber band tightly in both hands. Make this "plant stem" grow by stretching it.

TIGHT GRIP
PULL

How do plant cells grow according to this model?

Old cells grow larger throughout the "stem."

5 Hold the band tightly with one hand only. Make this "plant stem" grow by letting it slip through your other hand.

TIGHT GRIP
LOOSE
PULL

How do cells grow according to this model?

New cells form and grow at the left of the "stem."

6 Examine the plants you marked in your tray. Where do you see evidence of . . .

. . . new cells forming?

At the bean's tip and the corn's base.

. . . old cells stretching?

Along the upper bean stem.

7 Look at corn plants, both young and old. Summarize how they grow.

8 Look at bean plants, both young and old. Summarize how they grow.

END

Beans grow from the top. New stem and leaf cells continually form at the tip of the plant, building upon a foundation of older cells below.

The first leaves to form are a heart-shaped pair with large lobes. These developed from the original plumule on the seed embryo. They are the bean's only double leaves. As the stem continues to lengthen, it branches at intervals into 3 repeating parts: The first branch sends out a triplet of unlobed leaves; the second branch sends out a flower that will eventually form a bean pod and a new generation of seeds; the third branch is a continuation of the growing stem. (If your growing conditions are slow, these repetitions may not yet be observable.)

Corn grows from the bottom. New leaf cells continually form at the base, pushing older leaf cells ahead of them, through the coleoptile and out into sunlight.

Corn also grows from inside to outside. As old leaves mature, new leaves keep telescoping up from the center, gradually displacing the older leaves to the outside.

TEACHING NOTES

**Sprout mass

2. If you haven't removed the lid already, to give the sprouts extra growing room, consider doing it now. Throw away the towels, and stand the roots in about a centimeter of water.

*How plants grow

4. Plants grow because their individual cells grow. This stretching rubber band accurately models real growth because the cells grow longer in both cases. But the model breaks down when examining the width of the cells. The rubber band cells get thinner, whereas real plant cells actually grow thicker.

5. Old cells can't stretch indefinitely. New cells also need to form, through cell division, in order to sustain growth. In this model they are "dividing" as the rubber band slides through the thumb and forefinger of the right hand.

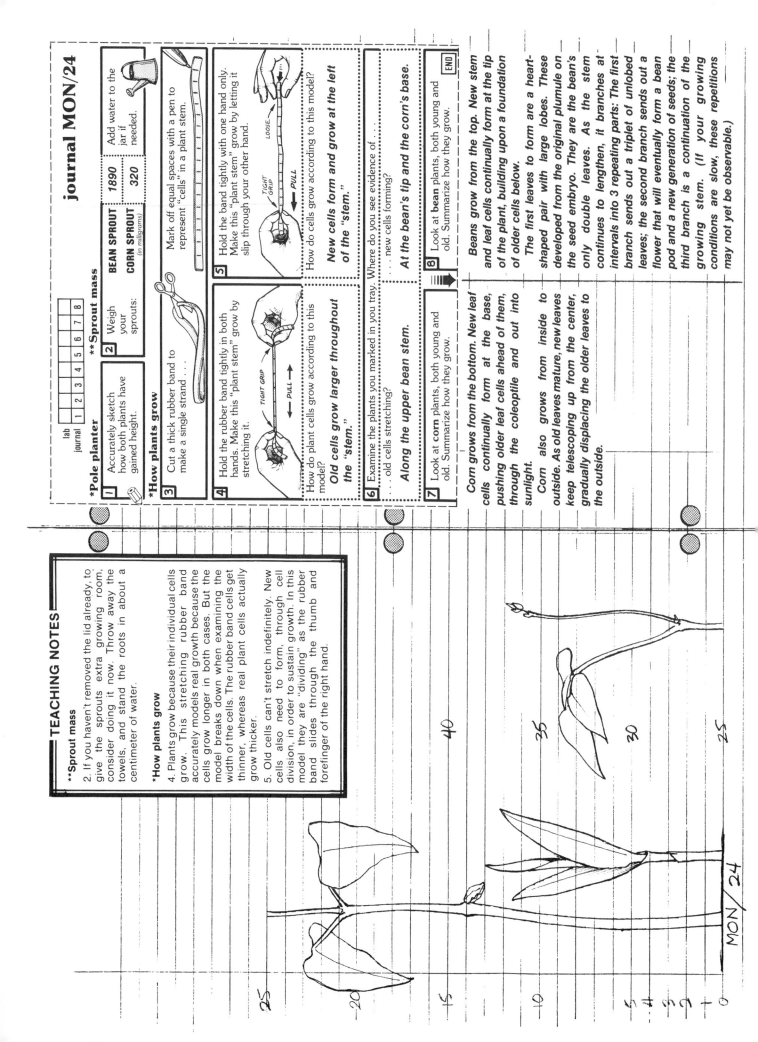

MON/24

journal TUE/25

🏠 LAB

BEAN SPROUT	1920
CORN SPROUT *(in milligrams)*	310

lab	3	4	5	6	7	8
journal	1	2				

*Pole planter

1 Accurately sketch how both plants have gained height. ✏️

**Sprout mass

2 Weigh your sprouts for the last time. Center your balance first.

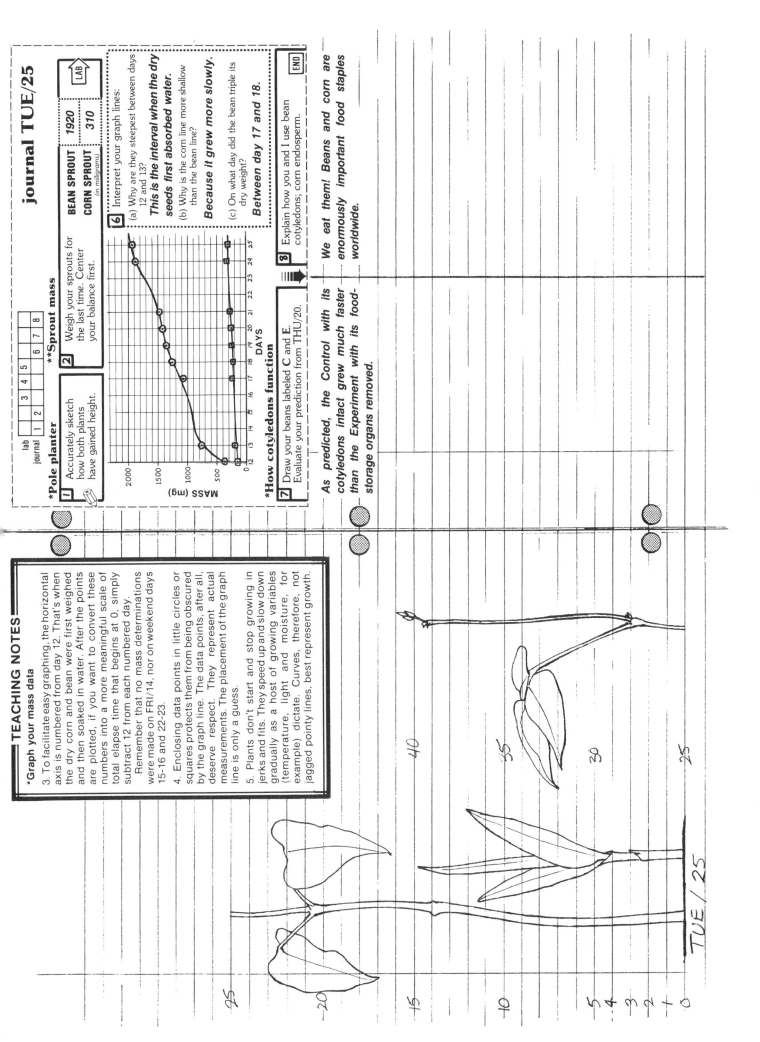

MASS (mg) — 2000, 1500, 1000, 500, 0

DAYS — 12 13 14 15 16 17 18 19 20 21 22 23 24 25

*How cotyledons function

7 Draw your beans labeled C and E. Evaluate your prediction from THU/20.

6 Interpret your graph lines:

(a) Why are they steepest between days 12 and 13?
This is the interval when the dry seeds first absorbed water.

(b) Why is the corn line more shallow than the bean line?
Because it grew more slowly.

(c) On what day did the bean triple its dry weight?
Between day 17 and 18.

END

8 Explain how you and I use bean cotyledons; corn endosperm.

As predicted, the Control with its cotyledons intact grew much faster than the Experiment with its food-storage organs removed.

We eat them! Beans and corn are enormously important food staples worldwide.

TEACHING NOTES

*Graph your mass data

3. To facilitate easy graphing, the horizontal axis is numbered from day 12. That's when the dry corn and bean were first weighed and then soaked in water. After the points are plotted, if you want to convert these numbers into a more meaningful scale of total elapse time that begins at 0, simply subtract 12 from each numbered day.

Remember that no mass determinations were made on FRI/14, nor on weekend days 15-16 and 22-23.

4. Enclosing data points in little circles or squares protects them from being obscured by the graph line. The data points, after all, deserve respect. They represent actual measurements. The placement of the graph line is only a guess.

5. Plants don't start and stop growing in jerks and fits. They speed up and slow down gradually as a host of growing variables (temperature, light and moisture, for example) dictate. Curves, therefore, not jagged pointy lines, best represent growth.

40

35

30

25

25

—20

15

10

5
4
3
2
1
0

TUE / 25

lab					
journal	1	2	3	4	5

*Pole planter

1 Sketch for the last time how your corn and bean plants have gained height. ✎

*Graph height data

2 Graph the daily height of your bean and corn plants, beginning at FRI/7. Use circles and squares as before, and connect them with smooth lines.

BEAN: ⊙   CORN: ⊡

Graph:

HEIGHT (paper lines) — vertical axis: 10, 20, 30, 40, 50
DAYS — horizontal axis: 9, 11, 13, 15, 17, 19, 21, 23, 25

Plants grow at widely variable rates depending on growing conditions. As rates increase, the steeper part of a growth curve forms. As growth slows again, the curve levels off, and so on. ✎

3 Living things grow in "s-curve" graph patterns. Explain why.

*Photosynthesis

4 Remove the foil and paper clip from your bean leaf and write your observations below . . . .

. . . then evaluate your prediction from FRI/14.

5 Observe the leaves greased on top, "T," and on bottom, "B."

Where are the stomata on a bean leaf? How do you know?

Hm-m-m...   Hm-m-m...

END

➤

The part of the leaf covered by foil has turned yellow. It lost its green color as predicted, because without sunlight, it was no longer able to photosynthesize.

The results suggest that stomata are located on the bottom side of bean leaves. First, the "B" leaf, greased on the bottom, is just starting to turn yellow. Apparently stomata were blocked on this surface by grease. Second, the "T" leaf, greased on the top, still remains fully green. Its stomata can only remain unblocked if located on the ungreased underside of the leaf.

TEACHING NOTES

*Graph your height data

2. Unlike the previous graph, this one measures the total elapsed time since the bean and corn were first exposed to moisture way back on FRI/0. The graph begins on the FRI/7 since that is the first day the height was recorded.

Again, students should skip weekends 8-9, 15-16, and 22-23 when no data was recorded.

*Photosynthesis

4-5. These experiments have been in progress for 12 days, since FRI/14. This is enough time to produce yellowing in the sunlight-deprived leaf that is covered by foil.

The leaf that is greased on the bottom, blocking intake of CO₂' through the stomata, will also yellow, but the effect is more subtle. Apparently leaves can survive a lack of CO₂' over a longer period of time than a lack of light, before the green chlorophyll is finally lost. If you leave at least one greased-leaf experiment in place after this module ends, for perhaps a week or 2 longer, this yellowing effect gradually becomes more apparent.

Be careful about generalizing from bean leaves to all leaves in general. Stomatal openings may also occur on the stems of many plants. And they don't always reside on the underside of leaves. Floating lily pads, for example, have stomatal openings that occur exclusively on the top of the leaves for obvious reasons.

Illustration labels along right margin: 25, 20, 15, 10, 5, 4, 3, 2, 1, 0

WED/26

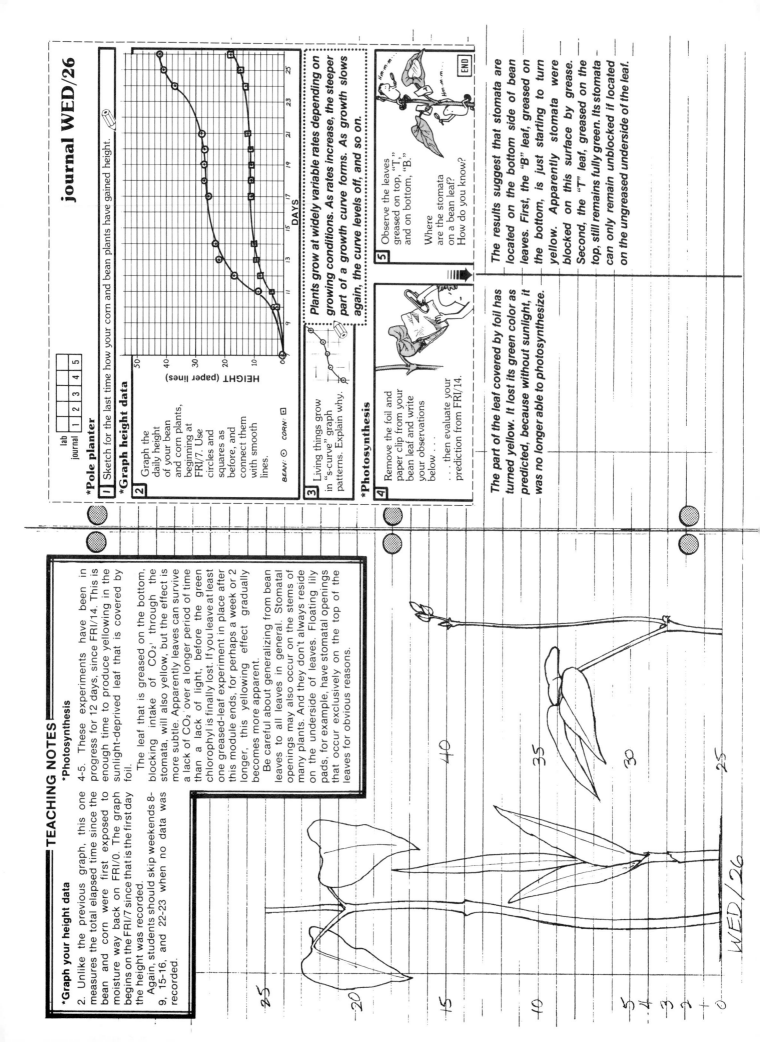

lab
journal 1 | 2

*Examine mature plants

1 This is how each plant looks when full grown. Label these parts:

CORN:
adventitious root
primary root
node
leaf
stalk
flower
fruit

BEAN:
primary root
secondary root
hypocotyl
first leaves
leaf triplet
node
stem
flower
pod

CORN:

FLOWER (male tassels)
FRUIT
leaf
STALK
NODE
FLOWER (female silk)
ADVENTITIOUS ROOTS
PRIMARY ROOT

BEAN:

FLOWER
LEAF TRIPLET
FIRST LEAVES
POD
STEM
HYPOCOTYL
SECONDARY ROOTS

ROOTS | STEMS
LEAVES | FLOWERS

END

2 Divide your 2 columns below into 4 boxes labeled ROOTS, STEMS, LEAVES and FLOWERS. Explain how plants use each part.

ROOTS:
These absorb water and minerals into the plant, anchor it firmly in the ground, and store food reserves derived from photosynthesis.

STEMS:
These provide a channel to transport water and minerals up from the roots and food reserves down from the leaves.

LEAVES:
These combine water and carbon dioxide in the presence of sunlight to photosynthesize food for the rest of the plant.

FLOWERS:
These reproduce the plant by forming the next generation of seeds.

TEACHING NOTES

*Examine mature plants

1. Invite at least 1 lab group to donate their pole planter and plant tray to your classroom, for continued informal observations in the weeks ahead. If mold doesn't overcome them first, the beans will complete their entire life cycle — from seed to sprout to mature plant to self-pollinating flowers to pod, and finally back to seed. Corn, unfortunately, doesn't have enough growing room to reach maturity.

2. To explain the function of stems and flowers, your students will have to rely on their own background knowledge and experience. If they need additional input, you might write brief definitions on the blackboard, or discuss stem and flower functions in advance.

JOURNAL EVALUATIONS

Today's schedule is light enough to give you time to grade journals. If you have initialed your approval of daily entries, as suggested in step 9 of MON/3, you can now total these approvals, while each student stands by, and quickly assign a final grade. Otherwise, you should collect all journals at the end of the period to evaluate and return. Ask students to check their journals for completeness before handing them in. Those who finish early might decorate their covers in crayon or colored pencil for extra credit.

Be sure to return all journals by tomorrow, FRI/28. Students will use these as references, as they complete their take-home tests. In addition, they will be eager to show family members how much they have accomplished over the last 4 weeks.

We recommend that journal grades comprise perhaps a third of each student's overall module grade. The take-home test might form another third, with daily work habits and attitude completing the final third.

SOAK LENTILS AND WHEAT BERRIES

Students will begin their take-home tests by finding the average mass of lentils and wheat berries, both dry and presoaked. This is a high priority, since tomorrow may be the last day that balances are still available to all students. Soak perhaps 150 wheat berries and 150 lentils now (6 big pinches each), between damp paper towels. Set aside until tomorrow.

CLEAN-UP

Decide now how you want to dispose of all the corn and beans growing in your classroom. Don't actually start cleaning up until *after* students have weighed their lentils and wheat berries on, FRI/28.

There are several advantages to composting the corn and beans in your school garden. It's quick and easy. You keep lab items that may prove useful later. Tomorrow's take-home test, for example, requires at least 1 baby food jar plus lid, for every student in class. If you haven't collected that many extra's in advance, you'll need to recycle jars that are now occupied by plants.

Here is another consideration. There is a trend away from styrofoam egg cartons towards more biodegradable cardboard. You may want to conserve the styrofoam egg cartons you have now, to recycle next time you teach this module. (Think about stockpiling new ones, as well.)

On the other hand, suppose you decide that your room is already too overstocked with jars and egg cartons. Perhaps your students are begging to take everything home.

To exercise this option, first ask lab pairs to decide who keeps the plant tray, the balance, etc. Then provide a large paper grocery bag to anyone who needs it. Direct students to cut the bag to size like this:

Line the bottom with 4 pieces cut from the top.

Strengthen the remaining sides by doubling to the inside.

Arrange equipment inside like this.

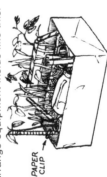

PAPER CLIP

Pour all water from the large jar, wringing excess water from the wicking towels that hang down. Notice how the pole planter is paper-clipped to the side of the bag so it can't tip over.

Dear Family Member,

Over the next 2 weeks, your child will study how seeds grow, applying concepts and skills already presented in class. Beyond paper towels and small jars, no special equipment is required.

Please participate; great leaps forward in learning could result! Keep in mind that this **is** a take-home test. Assist your child without directing; help your child to think and act independently.

Dear Student,

You are given wheat berries and lentils in a sealed baby food jar.

Your task is to find out all you can about each kind of seed by doing experiments; to report your findings in an organized way using complete sentences and detailed drawings.

You have 2 weeks. Do your best job. These instructions will help get you started.

TOPS Take-Home Test

1 Get a clean, dry baby food jar. Lightly wad a paper towel and push it inside.

2 Fold a second paper towel in half 4 times to make a small square.

{ 16 LAYERS }

3 Draw a circle on this square by tracing around the bottom of the jar.

4 Cut out the 16 layers of circles. Fit them on top of the crumpled towel.

5 Soak with water until the jar remains half full.

Never fill above ½.

½ —

6 Add 3 wheat berries and 3 lentils to the top. Close the lid and date the jar.

TODAY'S DATE

Will you sprout more seeds at another time? Will you transfer your best sprouts to other jars? Keep some seeds dry? Keep a daily journal? Will you begin writing observations and drawing sketches today?

What you do next, and how you do it, is all up to you. Here are **3 hints** to help you on your way:

THINK IT THROUGH....

??

a. When not looking at your seeds, keep the lid on. When the sprouts grow taller than the rim, it's O.K. to leave the lid off.

We have room to grow!

We're warm!

b. Set your sprouts near a window. When in direct sunlight, keep the lid off and the water level up.

Ah-h-h!

REFILL to ½

c. Use your balance to complete each equation.

10 dry lentils = ...mg
1 dry lentil = ...mg
10 dry wheat berries = ...mg
1 dry wheat berry = ...mg
10 soaked lentils = ...mg
1 soaked lentil = ...mg
10 soaked wheat berries = ...mg
1 soaked wheat berry = ...mg

TEACHING NOTES

BEGIN THE TAKE-HOME TEST

Follow these simple steps to prepare your class for a home study of lentils and wheat:

(1) Display dry lentils and wheat berries in labeled containers, as well as your presoaked seeds from yesterday.

(2) Distribute a take-home test to each student. Ask each lab group to complete the mass equations in part (c) at the end of this test, before doing anything else. You may need to present a blackboard review about moving the decimal point 1 place left to divide a number by 10.

If you don't have enough class time for students to make their own weight determinations, have them copy this data into box (c) of their test papers:

10 dry lentils =	480 mg
1 dry lentil =	48 mg
10 dry wheat berries =	310 mg
1 dry wheat berry =	31 mg
10 soaked lentils =	1020 mg
1 soaked lentil =	102 mg
10 soaked wheat berries =	400 mg
1 soaked wheat berry =	40 mg

(3) Put 1 big pinch each of dry lentils and wheat berries in a baby food jar and cover with a lid. (There are 20 to 30 seeds in a big pinch.) Distribute one to each student.

(4) Review the entire take-home test with your whole class. Discuss your performance expectations and answer any questions students may have. Establish a due date and hold to it.

CLEAN UP

Exercise the compost option or the take-home option as described in THU/27. Remember to keep at least a few bean plants if you wish to observe the formation of flowers and pods over the coming weeks.

EVALUATE THE TAKE-HOME TEST

Expect a variety of student output. Award grades based on total effort and quality of work. Following are some fruitful areas of investigation that parallel the journal work students have already completed:

● A periodic record, both written and visual, of how wheat and lentils develop over the 2 week period.

● Statements of comparison or contrast about dry seeds, moist seeds, germination, growth of sprouts, development of leaves and roots.

● A quantitative analysis of water absorbtion.

● The classification of wheat as a monocot and lentils as a dicot. Students should refer to similarities between wheat and corn; between lentils and beans.

● Experiments involving any of these topics: photosynthesis, the location of stomata on leaves, cell growth, graphing height as a function of time.

TYPICAL GROWTH of LENTILS and WHEAT:

(actual size)

DAY 0:

DAY 1:

DAY 3:

DAY 5:

(1/2 size)

DAY 10:

(1/2 size) **DAY 14:**

REPRODUCIBLE
STUDENT
ACTIVITY SHEETS

HOW TO REMOVE WORKSHEETS

Our pages are "perfect bound" in the same manner that single sheets of stationary are attached to a writing pad. Except our pages are glued more securely. You can open the pages of this book flat out in order to write on them and photocopy worksheets.

This does place unusual strain on the binding, however. With continued use, some pages will eventually fall out. When this begins to happen, don't rush out and buy a new book. Simply separate all the pages from their glued binding, punch them with a 3-holed punch and reassemble them into your own personal notebook.

To separate pages that are already loose, remove them one at a time from the book, just like pulling sheets off a note pad. To separate pages that are more firmly attached, carefully draw a sharp knife between the glued pages.

To remove loose pages . . .

Pull gently outward. Don't tear.

To remove firm pages . . .

Pull a sharp knife between pages.

**Make an egg carton seed tray

1 Cut away the bumps on an egg carton lid. Tape your name(s) to the side.

"SAW" WITH SCISSORS

2 Fold 2 paper towels in half 3 times lengthwise. They should be no wider than 2 fingers.

2 FINGERS WIDE

3 Push both towels halfway through the center hole. Set them in a widemouth jar filled with water.

TOWELS JUST TOUCH BOTTOM → ← WATER

4 Lay back 1 towel on each side. Fold a third in half to cover the entire bottom.

THIRD TOWEL

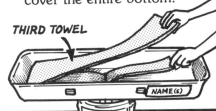

NAME(s)

5 Spread out 18 pinto beans and 9 corn in your tray. Cover with a fourth folded towel.

FOURTH TOWEL

NAME(s)

6 Soak with more water. Close the lid and set aside.

A sprout nursery!

*Make your plant journal

7 Get 12 journal cut-outs from your teacher.

8 Cut around the dashed lines into 23 separate parts:

journal MON/3

Count them!

. . . 19 WEEKDAYS . . .

. . . plus 4 PAPER MASSES.

journal MON/10

9 Paper clip the 4 paper masses together, and set aside.

10 Tape each weekday to a new sheet of notebook paper, even with the upper right corner.

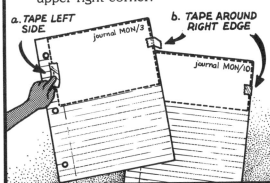

a. TAPE LEFT SIDE

b. TAPE AROUND RIGHT EDGE

journal MON/3

journal MON/10

11 Arrange all 19 journal days in order, beginning with MON/3. Add a cover sheet.

19 plus a cover.

journal TUE/4
journal MON/3

12 Tap the edges even. Staple very near each hole like this:

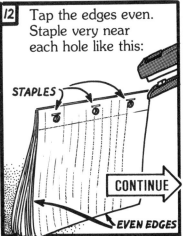

STAPLES

CONTINUE →

EVEN EDGES

13 Crease each page open along the spine, and extend the arrows.

Do all pages.

14 Write "PLANT JOURNAL" on the cover of your book. Put your name in the lower right corner.

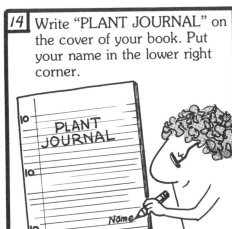

PLANT JOURNAL

Name

15 Paper clip your 4 **paper masses** to TUE/11 of your journal, near the bottom.

TUE/11

4 PAPER MASSES

END

lab MON/3

*Make a bean map

1 Cover this square with scratch paper. Carefully trace the square and the beans.

SCRATCH PAPER

2 Cut out your square. Fold it in the middle to make a stand-up "bean."

My BEAN MAP!

3 Choose an average-looking dry bean that has medium size and normal color.

Pretty ordinary...

4 **Carefully** draw all the tiny seed coat patterns on **both** sides of your special bean.

SAVE YOUR BEAN!

5 Mix your special bean together with 10 others. Use your map to find it again . . .

Can you find it in a group of 50?

6 Trade maps and beans with a friend . . .

Can your friend find the special 1 in 50?

**Soak some new seeds

7 Lift off the top paper towel from your seed tray. Wrap 5 dry beans and 5 dry corn inside.

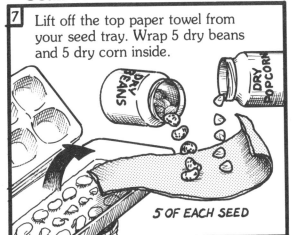

DRY BEANS

DRY POPCORN

5 OF EACH SEED

8 Set these new seeds back in your tray.

*Draw your sprouts

9 Find your most advanced bean and corn sprout. Draw both in your journal on the left page of MON/3.

journal MON/3

Include small details.

CONTINUE

10 Open your journal to MON/3 and read inside the big box.

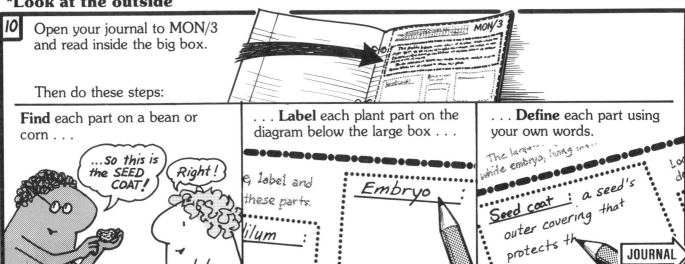

Then do these steps:

Find each part on a bean or corn . . .

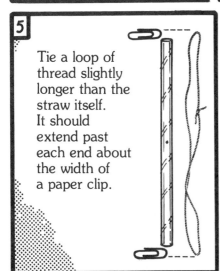

...So this is the SEED COAT!

Right!

. . . **Label** each plant part on the diagram below the large box . . .

e, label and these parts.

ilum

Embryo

. . . **Define** each part using your own words.

The larg... white embryo, living in...

Seed coat : a seed's outer covering that protects th

JOURNAL ➡

lab TUE/4

Build a balance

2 Wrap a plastic straw around a pencil so the ends meet exactly.

ENDS TOGETHER

3 Crease the exact center, then stick a pin through it.

CREASE ➡

✔ TEACHER CHECK

4 Pull the pin back out and straighten out the straw.

5 Tie a loop of thread slightly longer than the straw itself. It should extend past each end about the width of a paper clip.

6 Fold a small piece of masking tape over the center of your loop . . .

CENTER

. . . Tightly curl the tape so it easily slides through the straw.

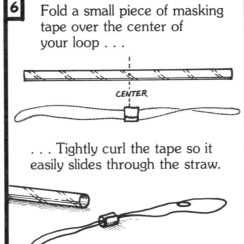

7 Feed your loop through the straw . . .

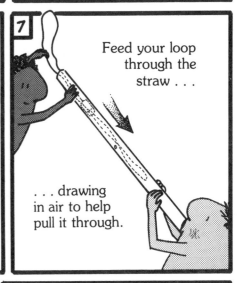

. . . drawing in air to help pull it through.

8 Center the thread inside its straw, so equal-sized loops hang out the ends.

⬅ EQUAL ➡

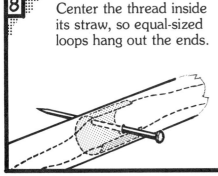

Poke your pin through the same center holes your made before, pushing through the masking tape inside.

9 Hang a paper clip on each loop so the ends point up.

END POINTS UP

CONTINUE ➡

10 Fold masking tape over the ends of a clothespin and pinch it flat . . .

Cut narrow center strips down to the wood. . .

CUT BOTH TABS

Scrape away these center strips to make "ears."

SCRAPE
SCRAPE

11 Tape your name(s) to the side of a can. Clip on the clothespin, then rest the straw and pin between.

SET PIN BETWEEN EARS

Name(s)

12 Trace this large dotted rectangle onto 2 pieces of foil.

Cut out both foil rectangles.

13 Fold 1 piece in half lengthwise . . .

Wrap it around a battery as shown . . .

FOLDED EDGE

BUMP END

HALF OFF BATTERY

14 Fold over the foil ends. Push the bottom flat on your table to make a "bucket.". .

FOLD OVER   PUSH FLAT

. . . remove the battery.

15 Make a second "bucket" as you did the first.

16 Hang each bucket from a paper clip on your balance beam.

17 Fold a small piece of masking tape almost in half . . .

STICKY END

Stick this "rider" on the high side of the straw so it balances level.

TO 18

**Compare wet and dry seeds

18 Unwrap the seed bundle and spread them out. Place dry seeds next to these for comparison.

Dry Beans   Dry Popcorn

DRY SEEDS

MOIST SEEDS   JOURNAL

22 Wrap up the moist seeds again. Return them to your tray.

**Make a storage mat

23 Divide and label a sheet of notebook paper like this:

EGG CARTON TRAY

JAR   BALANCE   POLE PLANTER

WRITE YOUR NAME(S)

24 Always store all your materials on this space-saving mat.

JAR

POLE PLANTER

END

**Make a pole planter

2 Pull up the middle of a paper clip . . .

. . . until you make it straight.

Wrap the big end in masking tape.

3 Roll up masking tape so it is sticky on the outside . . .

ABOUT THIS BIG

Stick it to the side of a baby food jar.

4 Stick the wrapped clip on top, then tape over all.

Write your name(s) on the tape.

Name(s)

5 Pull the free arm of the paper clip out just enough to fit a straw snugly over the top.

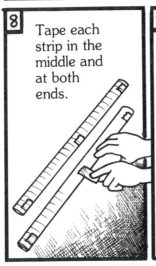

6 Trim 2 sheets of notebook paper along the top and bottom lines.

7 Fold these in half 4 times, to make narrow strips as wide as 1 little finger.

8 Tape each strip in the middle and at both ends.

9 Cut off half the straw you stuck onto your jar.

10 Use this piece to join both tubes of notebook paper together.

HALF STRAW

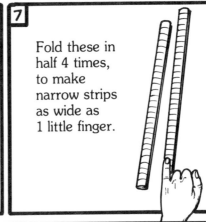

11 Number up this long strip (starting with "0") so each line runs through its number.

GAP

START FROM "0"

Number across the gap, too.

12 Stick this numbered strip over the half straw on your jar.

This makes a BEAN POLE!

13 Cut and fold masking tape lengthwise, as long as your index finger.

←FOLD

Make cuts from opposite sides about here:

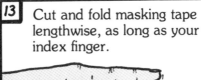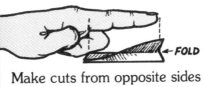

14 Tape it to the **back** of your pole at line 20:

TAPE

Tie up your bean after it grows.

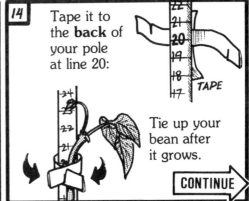

CONTINUE ➡

*Look at the inside

15 Unwrap the bundle of seeds in you tray.
Select an **un**sprouted bean and corn.

16 Hold your bean so its hilum faces away from you . . .

HILUM

Push your thumbnail through the seed coat, then gently pry the halves open like a book . . .

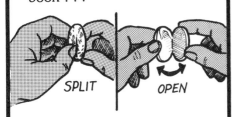

SPLIT   OPEN

Set the opened bean on your table.

17 Push a pin through the lower part of the corn embryo and force it through the bottom . . .

Pry this opening apart with your thumbnails . . .

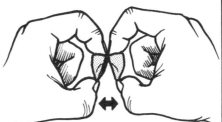

Set the opened corn on your table.

18 Open your journal to WED/5 and read inside the big box . . .

journal WED/5

Find each part on your opened seeds, **then** write descriptions underneath.

TWO COTYLEDONS . . .

YEAH !

JOURNAL ➤

lab THU/6

**Plant your pole planter

2 Cut a piece of paper towel about as big as this rectangle . . .

Roll it lengthwise into a tube, then moisten with water.

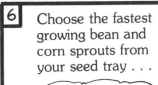

RUBBER BAND

Press it inside your pole planter like this. Hold it with a rubber band.

3 Fill with vermiculite.

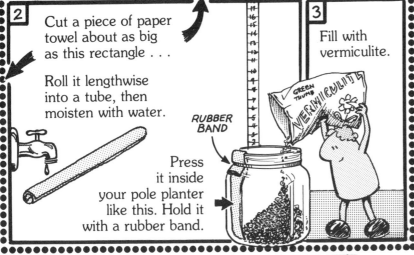

GREEN THUMB VERMICULITE

4 Add water, then drain completely.

5 Poke 2 deep pencil holes into the jar.

6 Choose the fastest growing bean and corn sprouts from your seed tray . . .

We're the champs!

Rest them in the holes so the tops **just** stick out.

*Look at growing sprouts

7 Open your journal to THU/6 and read inside the big box.

journal THU/6

Find each part on real sprouts **before** you write your descriptions.

JOURNAL ➤

*Prepare your journal for daily drawings

1 Open your journal to the **left** side of FRI/7.

2 Adjust your pole so "0" is even with the surface . . .

EVEN!

SURFACE

Draw a heavy line to represent this surface, and write "FRI/7" beneath. Number up the side from "0" to "5" so you divide each line.

FRI / 7

BOTTOM LEFT CORNER

3 Draw how far each sprout pokes above line "0" (the ground).

The bean is a little above the "0".

FRI/7

4 Draw similar "0" lines in the lower left corner of all remaining journal pages. Write the correct days, and number up the sides, as before.

Continue through WED/26.

TUE /11

MON /10

FRI /7

JOURNAL

**Plant your seed tray

4 Lift out the damp towel (with its sprouts) from your seed tray. Set it on your table.

5 Cut off the egg-cup side, so only the tray side remains.

LEAVE ON JAR

6 Reline with one new paper towel folded in half. Leave the 2 "wick" towels in place.

COVER THE HOLES

7 Gently pull your tallest bean plant from the towel and stand it in the corner of your tray. Cover the roots with enough **dry** vermiculite to hold it upright.

CAREFUL!

WHEW!

8 Cover the roots of more sprouts, one by one, until you arrange your 10 tallest plants like these.

Set aside the extras...

6 BEAN   4 CORN   EMPTY

1/2 TRAY   1/4 TRAY

FREE SPROUTS

CONTINUE

9 Add 6 dry beans and 3 dry corn to the open end.

10 Fill the whole tray brim full with vermiculite. Moisten with plenty of water.

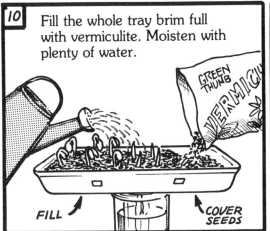

FILL

COVER SEEDS

GREEN THUMB VERMICU

11 Unbend 2 paper clips to right angles.

90°

Fix each to the bottom of the tray with masking tape.

...right against the jar...

12 Unbend 4 more paper clips to about this angle:

4 of these...

13 Cut a straw in half. Use 2 of the clips to join each half-straw to a whole middle straw.

PAPER CLIP   WHOLE STRAW   HALF STRAW

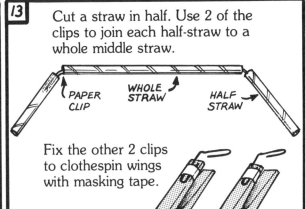

Fix the other 2 clips to clothespin wings with masking tape.

14 Clamp the clothespins to each end of your tray. Attach the straws to form an arch.

A plant support !

END

lab TUE/11

*Cut out your paper masses

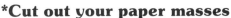

3 Get the paper masses clipped to your journal page. Cut out each one, staying exactly on the outside solid lines.

Be really careful!

4 Fold the 3 largest masses in half. Leave the smaller ones flat.

FOLD TO SHORTEN

1000 mg (1 gram)   1000 mg (1 gram)   500 mg

LEAVE OTHERS FLAT

5 Smash the right bucket on your balance flat, then rebalance it.

LEVEL

FLATTENED BUCKET

JOURNAL

lab WED/12

**Plant dry seeds

2 Push 4 dry beans and 2 dry corn deep into your tray, and cover them over.

**Number seeds and weigh them

3 Lay 4 more dry corn before you, with cotyledons **underneath.** Number each yellow endosperm with your pencil.

1   2
3   4

4 Number 4 dry beans by making these pencil marks on each hilum:

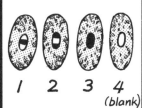
1   2   3   4 (blank)

5 Weigh each seed. Complete the table in your journal.

ALWAYS CENTER BEFORE STARTING

SEED   MASSES

JOURNAL

**Add water

2 Water your pole planter so the wick is moist . . .

moist...

. . . Refill the jar under your plant tray.

**Cover some bean leaves

3 Trace this square onto a piece of foil. Cut it out . . .

. . . then fold it into quarters.

4 Find a large bean leaf in your plant tray and slip the foil over it. Hold it on with a paper clip.

5 Divide a short piece of masking tape into 2 narrow strips. Label one "T" for top, the other "B" for bottom.

CUT LENGTHWISE.

T
B

6 Tag another pair of large bean leaves with each letter.

7 Smear some grease across **only** the bottom of leaf "B" and **only** the top of leaf "T."

ONE SIDE ONLY!

JOURNAL ▷

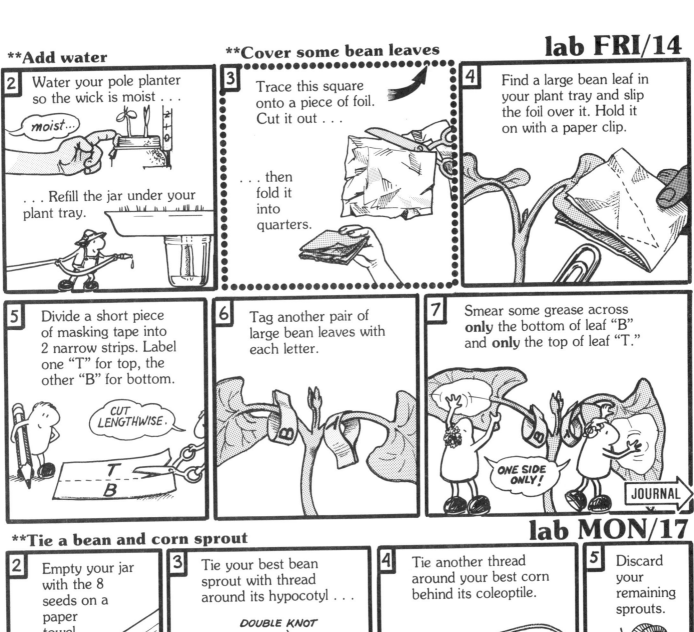

**Tie a bean and corn sprout

2 Empty your jar with the 8 seeds on a paper towel.

3 Tie your best bean sprout with thread around its hypocotyl . . .

DOUBLE KNOT

4 Tie another thread around your best corn behind its coleoptile.

Trim one end short; leave the other as long as your hand.

5 Discard your remaining sprouts.

m-m-m!

EXTRA SPROUTS

6 Fold a paper towel in half 2 times lengthwise . . .

. . . then tear it in half.

7 Moisten each half. Mold them over the rim of your empty jar so the ends reach to the bottom . . .

Fill 1/4 with water.

¼ —

8 Find the numbers you wrote on each sprout. Enter them in your journal table.

Looks like number 2...

JOURNAL ▷

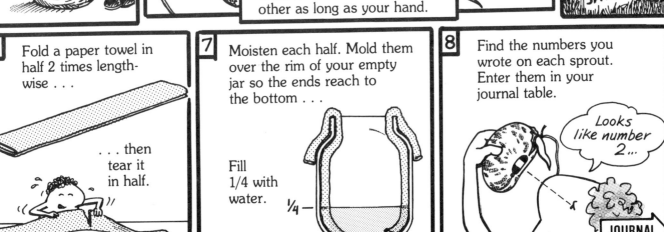

*Compare leaves

9 Remove a leaf from each uprooted plant to make pencil rubbings. Label each shape.

LEAVES UNDER PAPER
RUB LIGHTLY WITH SIDE OF LEAD
CORN

10 Draw the veins in darker, in careful detail. Store these drawings in your journal.

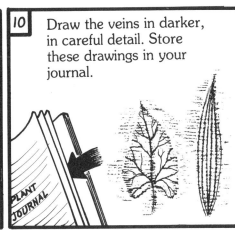

PLANT JOURNAL

11 Assignment: Bring more leaves of each type to pencil-rub tomorrow.

PARALLEL VEINS:
BRANCHING VEINS:
Please remember!
END

**Study cotyledons

3 Divide a short piece of masking tape lengthwise. Label one "E" for experiment, the other "C" for control.

E
C

4 Find 2 young bean sprouts of equal size, with newly opened cotyledons. Tag each plant around its base.

E   C

5 Gently break off the cotyledons from "E" only. Set them in the box labeled "YOUNG cotyledons" in your journal.

sorry!   !
E   C
JOURNAL

**Study plant growth

4 Cut a square of notebook paper exactly 4 lines long, and as wide as the margin.

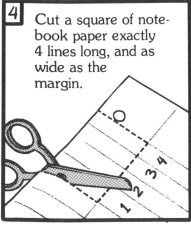

1 2 3 4

5 Tape a pin over the middle line so its "head and neck" clear the edge.

6 Fold in on the outside lines to make the paper exactly 2 lines wide.

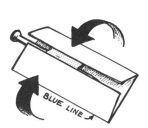

BLUE LINE

7 Put **one** drop of blue food coloring into a lid for dipping.

JOURNAL

*Graph your mass data

3 Graph the daily mass of your bean and corn plants. Begin with the table on MON/17.

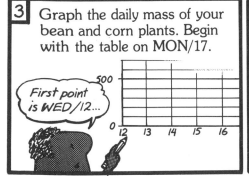

First point is WED/12...
500
0
12 13 14 15 16

4 Circle each bean point. Draw a square around each corn point.

BEAN: ⊙   CORN: ▣

5 Draw the best smooth curve you can through the data points.

Don't draw inside squares and circles.
JOURNAL

lab	1	2	3	4	5	6	7	8	9	10		
journal											11	12

journal MON/3

The **BEAN** is covered by a speckled **seed coat**. It protects the plant embryo, wrapped inside, from insects and water loss. The scar where the bean was once attached to its pod is called the **hilum**. Next to the hilum is a tiny hole called the **micropyle**. The embryo absorbs water most rapidly through this opening.

The largest part of the **CORN** is a yellow fruit called the **endosperm**. It is a food source for the white **embryo**, living inside, that will grow into a corn plant.

Locate, label and define these parts.

Seed coat :

_____ :

_____ :

_____ :

_____ :

EXTEND LINES DOWN
FROM ALL ARROWS

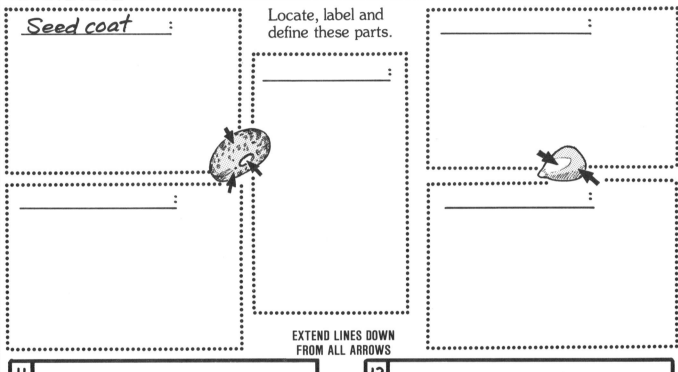

11 List below 4 ways your dry bean and corn seeds are **different**.

12 List 4 ways your dry bean and corn seeds are **similar**. END

lab				4	5	6	7	8	9	10	11	12	13	14
journal	1	2	3											

journal MON/10

*Pole planter

1 Get your pole planter. On the left page, carefully draw how high both seedlings now reach up the pole.

2 Next to your drawing, explain why the bean's **hypocotyl** forms a hook; why the corn's leaves hide inside a **coleoptile**.

LIKE A HOOK: LEAVES INSIDE:

*Draw your sprouts

3 Accurately draw your most advanced bean and corn sprout in the space below. Label all parts.

FASTEST GROWING!

LABEL ALL PARTS...

CORN:

BEAN: LAB

*Draw your sprouts

journal TUE/4

1 Draw your fastest-growing bean and corn sprout on the left page. **LAB**

19 Compare the mass of dry seeds to soaked seeds on your balance, then complete each equation:

ALWAYS CENTER FIRST

5 soaked beans = ☐ **dry beans**

5 soaked corn = ☐ **dry corn**

20 Draw in these boxes the differences you notice:

DRY BEAN → SOAKED BEAN

DRY CORN → SOAKED CORN

21 Describe these before/after changes, using **complete** sentences.

DRY ... **before** adding water	**WET** ... **after** 24 hours

SIZE

BEAN:	BEAN:
CORN:	CORN:

COLOR

BEAN:	BEAN:
CORN:	CORN:

TEXTURE

BEAN:	BEAN:
CORN:	CORN:

LAB

lab		2	3	4	5	6	7	8	9	10	11	12	13	14	15	16	17	18		
journal	1																		19	20

**journal
WED/5**

Draw your sprouts

I Draw your fastest-growing bean and corn sprout on the left page.

LAB ▷

The **BEAN** embryo easily breaks apart into **two cotyledons**. These store starch and protein, enabling the **plumule** to grow into the first 2 true leaves and the **radicle** to develop into the roots and lower stem.

The white **CORN** embryo does not divide easily because it has only **one cotyledon**. It absorbs starch and protein that is stored in the yellow **endosperm** for growth and development.

"MONO" means "ONE"... "DI" means "TWO."

19 Which seed above is called a **"monocot"** (monocotyledon)? Explain.

20 Which seed is called a **"dicot"** (dicotyledon)? Explain.

END

PAPER MASS:

500 mg

*Draw your sprouts

I Draw your fastest-growing bean and corn sprout on the left page.

LAB →

The lower half of the **BEAN** radicle develops into a complete root system: The **primary root** first grows down into the ground seeking moisture. The hard **root cap** at the tip protects it from being torn apart as it pushes through the soil. Tiny tubes called **root hairs**, just visible along the sides, absorb extra water. These are soon replaced by branching **secondary roots** that absorb water and anchor the plant firmly in the soil. With the root system in place, the **hypocotyl** directly above lengthens into a lower stem, pulling its **two cotyledons** through the soil into open sunlight.

CORN also develops a **primary root**, **root cap** and **root hairs** similar to the bean. Then the **coleoptile** pushes up from its **one cotyledon**. It forms a hollow protective tube that encloses the leaves safely inside until they can grow above ground. Meanwhile, **adventitious roots** grow form the base of the coleoptile to further support the plant and absorb water.

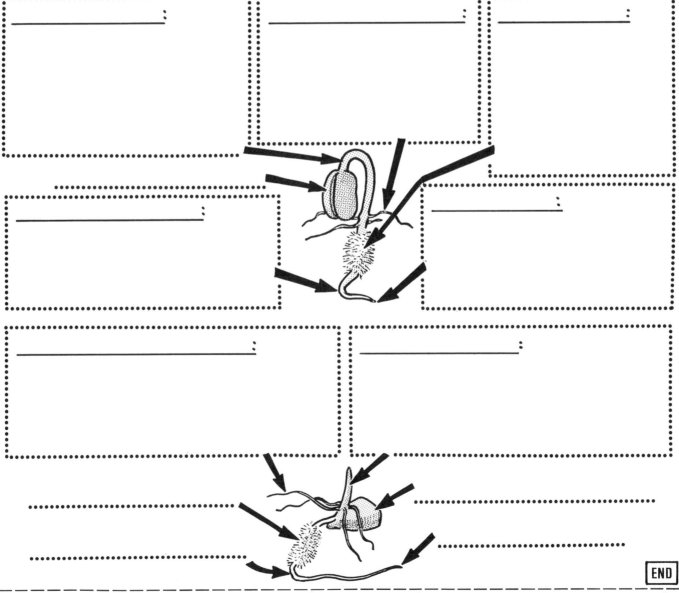

END

lab	1	2	3	4							
journal					5	6					

*The week in review

5 Divide your FRI/7 pages into 5 boxes labeled A, B, C, D and E, like this:

6 Summarize how your bean and corn looked at each stage:

ACCURATE DRAWINGS

NEW VOCABULARY

A. Dry seeds:

z-z-z-z

B. Water absorbed:

Even my toes are wrinkled!

C. Just sprouting:

Happy Birthday! Thanks!

D. Root hairs first form:

ROOTS!

E. Right now:

Any secondary roots?

Nope... Yep!

END

---

lab			3	4	5						
journal	1	2				6	7	8	9	10	11

*Pole planter

1 Accurately sketch how both plants have gained height.

**Sprout mass

2 Weigh your sprouts on your centered balance.

BEAN SPROUT
CORN SPROUT

LAB

(in milligrams)

YOUNG cotyledons:

OLD cotyledons:

6 Tell how bean plants use their cotyledons. (See WED/5 in your journal.)

7 Draw how your experiment and control look right **now**.

8 Predict how they will continue to develop.

9 Pinch the cotyledons off the most advanced bean plant in your tray (not used in another experiment) and set them in the "OLD" box above.

10 How do young cotyledons look different from older ones? Propose a theory to explain this difference.

11 Weigh both pairs of cotyledons on your balance. How do these results support your theory?

END

*Pole planter

1 On the left of this page, draw how high both seedlings now reach up the pole planter.

2 Divide the 2 columns you drew below into 4 boxes, labeled A, B, C and D. Answer each of these questions in its own box.

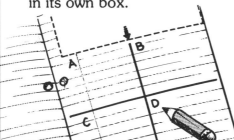

A. Observe your growing plants. Do they grow straight up, or lean in a favored direction? Make a drawing.

B. Propose a theory to explain your observations.

C. How might you test your theory?

LAB ▷

**Weigh a seed

6 Weigh a dry bean and corn on you balance. Tell how you did this in box **D** below.

7 Store all paper masses inside the can.

END

*Examine mature plants

1 This is how each plant looks when full grown. Label these parts:

adventitious root
primary root
node
leaf
stalk
flower
fruit

primary root
secondary root
hypocotyl
first leaves
leaf triplet
node
stem
flower
pod

CORN:

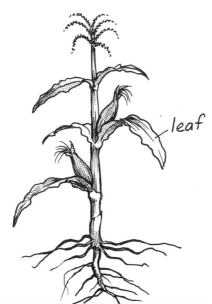

leaf

BEAN:

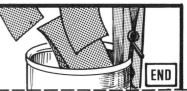

2 Divide your 2 columns below into 4 boxes labeled ROOTS, STEMS, LEAVES and FLOWERS. Explain how plants use each part.

END

*Pole planter

1 On the left page, draw each pole plant exactly as you see it—like a snapshot. **LAB**

TABLE:

	#1	#2	#3	#4	TOTAL	AVERAGE
DRY BEAN						
DRY CORN						

. . .all data in milligrams

6 After you weigh all 8 seeds, soak them overnight under water.

7 Do you think the seeds will gain weight by tomorrow? Explain.

8 Based on your observations of TUE/4, which seeds will likely gain the most? **END**

---

lab								
journal	1	2	3	4	5	6	7	8

journal MON/24

*Pole planter

1 Accurately sketch how both plants have gained height.

**Sprout mass

2 Weigh your sprouts:

BEAN SPROUT

CORN SPROUT (in milligrams)

Add water to the jar if needed.

*How plants grow

3 Cut a thick rubber band to make a single strand . . .

Mark off equal spaces with a pen to represent "cells" in a plant stem.

4 Hold the rubber band tightly in both hands. Make this "plant stem" grow by stretching it.

TIGHT GRIP

PULL

How do plant cells grow according to this model?

5 Hold the band tightly with one hand only. Make this "plant stem" grow by letting it slip through your other hand.

TIGHT GRIP   LOOSE

PULL

How do cells grow according to this model?

6 Examine the plants you marked in you tray. Where do you see evidence of . . .

. . . old cells stretching?

. . . new cells forming?

7 Look at **corn** plants, both young and old. Summarize how they grow.

8 Look at **bean** plants, both young and old. Summarize how they grow. **END**

*Pole planter   **Weigh soaked seeds

1 Draw each pole plant exactly as you see it. Your sketch should always show the height of leaves **and** cotyledons.

2 Complete this table. Use your balance, plus data from WED/12:

	#1	#2	#3	#4	Total	Average
SOAKED BEAN						
DRY BEAN						
Water Absorbed						
SOAKED CORN						
DRY CORN						
Water Absorbed						

. . .all data in milligrams

3 Fold a **wet** paper towel into the bottom of a baby food jar, and set your 8 seeds on top.

Tape on your name. Cover tightly and set aside until MON/17.

NAME(s)

4 Use data from your table to compare how beans and corn absorb water. Was your prediction from WED/12 a good one?

5 How many beans are needed to absorb 250 grams of water? (1 gram = 1000 mg)

250 mg   one glass full!

END

*Pole planter   **Sprout mass

1 Accurately sketch how both plants have gained height.

2 Weigh your sprouts on a centered balance.

BEAN SPROUT

CORN SPROUT
(in milligrams)

Add water to the jar if needed.

*Monocots and Dicots

3 Cut out the rubbings you made yesterday. Tape each into the correct column below.

CUT:

TAPE

4 Make rubbings of other leaves you have collected, and draw in the veins. Cut and tape them below.

5 Draw arrows to show where the cotyledons are located on these seeds:

RICE GRAIN   PEANUT

Predict what kind of leaves each seed will produce:

MONOCOT LEAVES: **DICOT LEAVES:**   END

*Pole planter

1 Accurately draw on the left page how both plants have gained height. ✏ **LAB ▶**

8 Leaves turn green in sunlight as they use the sun's energy to photosynthesize their own food.

Green!

Predict the color of your leaf after being covered for a long time with foil. Explain your reasons.

9 Leaves breathe in air through tiny openings (stomata) in their leaves. Stomata are too small to see without a microscope.

CO_2

O_2

If grease plugs these holes, the leaves can't breathe. How might this experiment tell us where the stomata are located?

END

lab		2	3	4	5	6	7	8			
journal	1								9	10	11

journal MON/17

*Pole planter **Sprout mass

1 Accurately draw how both plants have grown.

LAB ▶

9 Complete this mass table. Be sure to center your balance first . . .

		DRY WED/12	SOAKED THU/13	SPROUTED MON/17
BEAN	#			
CORN	#			

(milligrams)

Return both sprouts to their jar so each leans against the damp towel. Keep water in the bottom; the lid tightly closed.

10 How much **more** mass did each seed gain after the 24-hour soak of THU/13?

11 What **other** way can seedlings gain mass besides absorbing water? **END**

PAPER MASS:

1000 mg (1 gram)

lab									9	10	11
journal	1	2	3	4	5	6	7	8			

journal TUE/18

*Pole planter

1 Accurately sketch how both plants have gained height.

**Sprout mass

2 Weigh each sprout you tied with thread.

BEAN SPROUT
CORN SPROUT
(in milligrams)

Return them to their jar and close the lid.

**Compare roots

3 Gently uproot a young bean and corn plant from your tray. Rinse off the roots.

CAREFUL!

4 Divide your columns below into boxes labeled 5, 6, 7 and 8. Do each step in its own box.

5 Sketch the bean's root system. Use this key:

PRIMARY ROOT
SECONDARY ROOT

BEAN

6 Sketch the corn's root system. Use this key:

PRIMARY ROOT
SECONDARY ROOT
ADVENTITIOUS ROOT

CORN

LIKE THESE!

7 Describe how these root systems are similar.

8 Describe how these root systems are different.

LAB

---

*Pole planter

1 Accurately sketch how both plants have gained height.

**Sprout mass

2 Weigh your sprouts for the last time. Center your balance first.

BEAN SPROUT
CORN SPROUT
(in milligrams)

LAB

6 Interpret your graph lines:

(a) Why are they steepest between days 12 and 13?

(b) Why is the corn line more shallow than the bean line?

(c) On what day did the bean triple its dry weight?

MASS (mg)
2000
1500
1000
500
0
12 13 14 15 16 17 18 19 20 21 22 23 24 25
DAYS

*How cotyledons function

7 Draw your beans labeled **C** and **E**. Evaluate your prediction from THU/20.

8 Explain how you and I use bean cotyledons; corn endosperm.

END

journal FRI/21

*Pole planter   ****Sprout mass**   ****Add water**

1 Accurately sketch how both plants have gained height.

2 Weigh your sprouts. Remember to center your balance before you begin.

BEAN SPROUT ☐

CORN SPROUT ☐
(in milligrams)

3 Add water to your pole planter, plant tray, and sprout jar for the weekend.

LAB ▷

8 This "corn plant" has been marked with food coloring dots 1 line apart. Practice marking the "bean stem" in the same way with your pin and food coloring.

BEAN: **CORN:**

9 As both plants continue to grow, predict how each section will change (or not change). Give reasons for each answer.

a. tip-top of bean:

b. upper bean stem:

c. tip of new leaf to mid-coleoptile:

d. lower coleoptile:

10 Mark a bean and corn plant in your tray that look similar to the drawings above.

11 On the left, draw how your plants look **now**.

12 On the right, draw how they will look **later**, based on your predictions above.

NOW: *Show the dots.* ⬇   **LATER:**   END

PAPER MASSES: 10 mg | 20 mg | 30 mg | 50 mg

100 mg | 200 mg | 200 mg

lab journal | 1 | 2 | 3 | 4 | 5

*Pole planter

1 Sketch for the last time how your corn and bean plants have gained height.

*Graph height data

2 Graph the daily height of your bean and corn plants, beginning at FRI/7. Use circles and squares as before, and connect them with smooth lines.

BEAN: ⊙   **CORN:** ⊡

HEIGHT (paper lines)

50 — 40 — 30 — 20 — 10 — 0

7   9   11   13   15   17   19   21   23   25

DAYS

3 Living things grow in "s-curve" graph patterns. Explain why.

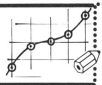

*Photosynthesis

4 Remove the foil and paper clip from your bean leaf and write your observations below . . .

. . . then evaluate your prediction from FRI/14.

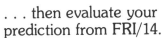

5 Observe the leaves greased on top, "T," and on bottom, "B."

Where are the stomata on a bean leaf? How do you know?

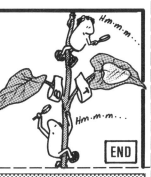

END

PAPER MASS:

1000 mg (1 gram)

<table>
<tr><td>

Dear Family Member,

Over the next 2 weeks, your child will study how seeds grow, applying concepts and skills already presented in class. Beyond paper towels and small jars, no special equipment is required.

Please participate; great leaps forward in learning could result! Keep in mind that this **is** a take-home test. Assist your child without directing; help your child to think and act independently.

</td><td>

Dear Student,

You are given wheat berries and lentils in a sealed baby food jar.

Your task is to find out all you can about each kind of seed by doing experiments; to report your findings in an organized way using complete sentences and detailed drawings.

You have 2 weeks. Do your best job. These instructions will help get you started.

</td></tr>
</table>

TOPS Take-Home Test

1 Get a clean, dry baby food jar. Lightly wad a paper towel and push it inside.

2 Fold a second paper towel in half 4 times to make a small square.

16 LAYERS

3 Draw a circle on this square by tracing around the bottom of the jar.

4 Cut out the 16 layers of circles. Fit them on top of the crumpled towel.

5 Soak with water until the jar remains half full.

Never fill above ½.

½ —

6 Add 3 wheat berries and 3 lentils to the top. Close the lid and date the jar.

TODAY'S DATE

?? THINK IT THROUGH...

Will you sprout more seeds at another time? Will you transfer your best sprouts to other jars? Keep some seeds dry? Keep a daily journal? Will you begin writing observations and drawing sketches today?

What you do next, and how you do it, is all up to you.
Here are **3 hints** to help you on your way:

a. When not looking at your seeds, keep the lid on. When the sprouts grow taller than the rim, it's O.K. to leave the lid off.

We're warm!

We have room to grow!

REFILL to ½

b. Set your sprouts near a window. When in direct sunlight, keep the lid off and the water level up.

Ah·h·h!

c. Use your balance to complete each equation.

10 dry lentils = ... mg
1 dry lentil = ... mg
10 dry wheat berries = ... mg
1 dry wheat berry = ... mg
10 soaked lentils = ... mg
1 soaked lentil = ... mg
10 soaked wheat berries = ... mg
1 soaked wheat berry = ... mg

FEEDBACK

If you enjoyed teaching TOPS please say so. Your praise will motivate us to work harder. If you found an error or can suggest ways to improve this module, we need to hear about that too. Your criticism will help us improve our next new edition. Do you need information about our other publications? We'll send you our latest catalog free of charge.

For whatever reason, we'd love to hear from you. We include this self-mailer for your convenience.

Ron and Peg Marson
author and illustrator

──────────────Your Message Here:──────────────

Module Title_____ Date _____

Name _____

Address _____

City_____ State_____ Zip_____

RETURN ADDRESS

_____

_____

_____

PLACE
STAMP
HERE

TOPS Learning Systems
10970 S. Mulino Road
Canby OR 97013

TAPE HERE